DIGITAL MAKEOVER

BÉATRICE COLLIN
MARIE TAILLARD

DIGITAL MAKEOVER

HOW **L'ORÉAL** PUT PEOPLE FIRST TO
BUILD A **BEAUTY TECH POWERHOUSE**

WILEY

Published by John Wiley & Sons, Inc., Hoboken, New Jersey.

Published simultaneously in Canada.

For general information on our other products and services or for technical support, please contact our Customer Care Department within the United States at (800) 762-2974, outside the United States at (317) 572-3993 or fax (317) 572-4002.

Wiley publishes in a variety of print and electronic formats and by print-on-demand. Some material included with standard print versions of this book may not be included in e-books or in print-on-demand. If this book refers to media such as a CD or DVD that is not included in the version you purchased, you may download this material at http://booksupport.wiley.com. For more information about Wiley products, visit www.wiley.com.

Library of Congress Cataloging-in-Publication Data is Available:

ISBN 978-1-119-70610-6 (Paperback)

ISBN 978-1-119-70608-3 (ePDF)

ISBN 978-1-119-70601-4 (ePub)

Cover Design: Wiley
Cover Image: © VPanteon/Getty Images
Author Photos: courtesy of the Authors

SKY10023933_010821

Contents

Foreword: Permanent Reinvention in the Genes...... ix

Introduction: Building a Beauty Powerhouse........ xiii

PART I Four Foundational Pillars..................... 1

1 Orchestrate Creativity........................3

    The Importance of an Evangelist............................4

    Time to Improvise...6

    From Creative Chaos to Orchestrated Rigor 13

    Enabling Resonance......................................16

2 Cultivate Healthy Doubt.....................21

    Productive Anxiety.......................................22

    Challenging the Status Quo 23

    Permanent Questioning 24

    The Dual Innovation Channel..............................25

    Balancing Passion with Science 26

    Tensions and Achievements 27

    Market Leader and Challenger.............................28

3 Learn and Innovate with Rigor.....................37

    Innovators Are Most Valuable Players 39

    Do, Undo, and Redo 42

    Incubators as Promoters of Change 47

4 Listen with Curiosity.............................51

    Politeness of the Heart 54

    Seizing What's Emerging..................................59

    L'Oréalization 60

Full Color Palette 61

Ban the Boring 64

An Open Innovation Ecosystem 65

PART II **A Human-Centered Transformation** **71**

5 **Centering Customers** 73

A Focus Shift 75

Precision Marketing 80

Seamless Customer Journeys 81

The Strategic Use of Data 84

6 **Becoming Social** 89

Social Centricity 92

Friends Find Solutions 94

Friends Give Advice 95

Friends Take You Places 96

Friends Share Their Looks 97

Friends Shop with You 98

Friends Stick Together 100

7 **Transforming Relationships with Partners** 105

From a Chain to an Ecosystem 106

Ecosystems' Key Attributes 108

Ecosystems Perform in Times of Crisis 114

8 **Putting People First** 119

Teams Are the New Heroes 122

Customer Satisfaction Is the New Product Performance 124

Eat What You Cook Is the New Leave Before It Burns 125

Frame and Trust Is the New Control .128

Problem-Solving Together Is the New Meeting Behavior 130

Empowerment Is the New Management 132

Test and Learn Is the New Perfection 133

Cooperation Is the New Confrontation. 135

Conclusion 139

Acknowledgments 143

About the Authors 147

**Appendix 1: L'Oréal's History: A Timeline
of Significant Dates** 151

**Appendix 2: Timeline of L'Oréal's Acquisitions
and Strategies** 153

**Appendix 3: A Selection of L'Oréal Brands
by Category 2020** 159

Appendix 4: Global Beauty Industry Data 161

Notes 167

References 175

Index 183

Foreword: Permanent Reinvention in the Genes

Over the last ten years, the pace and intensity of change have increased like never before. Everywhere, the world has been transformed at dizzying speeds. And as I write this preface, the current COVID-19 crisis is further accelerating these massive shifts, especially those related to digital.

With advances in science and technology, the digital tsunami that has seeped into all spheres of life, and the environmental and societal changes, we're experiencing a veritable Big Bang that has shattered our landmarks. From consumer behavior to marketing, distribution, and competition, a new world has emerged:

- A world whose only permanence has become movement
- A world that is volatile, uncertain, complex, and even more demanding
- A world where metamorphosis has become vital for companies

This unprecedented situation is undoubtedly the biggest upheaval of my entire career.

In more than forty years at L'Oréal, I thought I had already been exposed to the greatest shocks: I had been appointed head of our Asia zone one month before the Asian crisis of 1997, and head of North America a few days before September 11, 2001. And when I took over as Group CEO in 2006, I was almost immediately confronted with the crisis of 2008, which has been, in the end, an opportunity to redefine the company's major fundamentals:

- Its mission: beauty for all
- Its strategy: universalization (i.e. globalization) while respecting differences
- Its self-renewed objective: the conquest of a billion additional consumers

But a redefinition was no longer sufficient after the titanic changes of the last few years. They required a revolution, a full "reset" of our hard drive.

We've carried out our "revolutions" on three fronts, almost simultaneously:

- The digital revolution, which started in 2010, is widely described in this book so I will spare the fine details here. The COVID crisis has only deepened and quickened the digital wave. Everywhere, e-commerce is exploding. It will be the big winner from the crisis, as many consumers have experienced the convenience of purchasing online and will not go back. Its potential is immense and global. Thanks to online commerce that facilitates the delivery of products to even the most remote areas, the democratization of beauty will boost the market for many years to come. Additionally, consumers are developing stronger relationships with their favorite brands thanks to the internet and social networks. Today, on top of the digital revolution, winning the battle of Beauty Tech is vital. Our ambition is to be the undisputed world leader in Beauty Tech. This is the mission of the next few years, the one that will, once again, give us the edge over our competitors.

- The sustainable revolution launched in 2013 with our Sharing Beauty With All program. Since then, we have fundamentally shifted our paradigm, revolutionized our business model, and reinvented our approach in all areas of the company. We added sustainability as a criterion in product design, alongside quality and profitability. We have rethought procurement and production with new processes to reduce our footprint. We have largely "decarbonized" our production and proved that it is possible to decouple economic growth and environmental impact. For all of us, the pandemic crisis is a wake-up call to rebuild a greener economy with greater solidarity and cohesion. The environmental and social emergency is such that if we do not act, we will forsake our own future. This is why last June we launched our new L'Oréal for the Future program, with which we are committing to a new sustainable and inclusive revolution. The two are inseparable.

- Finally, we have been carrying out a cultural and managerial revolution that started in 2016. We are committed to our Simplicity program to transform the way we work and respond to the new expectations and aspirations of our employees. We're improving our daily working experience through better meetings, increased cooperation, cross-functionality, and a culture of constructive feedback. This leads to renewed relationships with work and management.

Each of these revolutions has helped us navigate the company through the great ruptures and shifts of the twenty-first century. What makes each of these revolutions so successful? First and foremost, L'Oréal's ability to reinvent itself.

For me, one of the strengths of this book is that it seeks to find, within the L'Oréal cultural genome, the springs of its continual adaptation, its agility, and its responsiveness. This is also the reason why I wanted to preface it.

Because the history of L'Oréal is one of constant reinvention. This capacity to reinvent ourselves is part of our genetic map. Generation after generation, our company has always known how to transform itself, to adapt, while remaining faithful to our founding principles and identity.

It is this permanent contrast that produces the originality of our business and cultural model. This "simultaneity," where long-term vision meets short-term pragmatism, helps create a group that is strategic in its course, mission, and objectives while pragmatic in its tactics and approach.

Central to L'Oréal's culture of consistent renewal are our extraordinary teams. Our employees combine unparalleled commitment and a constant pursuit of excellence with the ability to permanently reinvent themselves.

Each of L'Oréal's five chairmen in 110 years has had to face major upheavals to their environment and seize the opportunities they offered. Every leader has shown an obsessive desire to transform the company into each "new world."

Eugène Schueller initiated the scientific and industrial adventure at the beginning of the twentieth century. François Dalle led the "thirty glorious years" in France and Europe and the birth of mass distribution. Charles Zviak championed scientific and research innovation. Lindsay Owen-Jones piloted globalization. And I helped usher in the transformations at the dawn of the twenty-first century: the rise of China and Asia, the digital revolution, and the advent of social and environmental responsibility.

Permanent transformation is, for me, the only compass in our modern world, a world with chronic volatility and uncertainty that makes it more demanding but also incredibly stimulating. By following this compass, L'Oréal has been able to achieve sustainable growth for more than 110 years without ever denying its past.

This ability to reinvent itself has, in my opinion, become *the* true performance criterion for companies, if not the means of survival.

I have always sought to maintain this "L'Oréalian" culture of challenging the "status quo," which I have borne for the last fifteen years.

And when I look to the future, I am extremely confident.

Confident because beauty is a universal human aspiration that will continue to drive the cosmetics market.

Confident also because L'Oréal is perfectly equipped to be the beauty champion of the future; beauty enhanced by technology and digital capabilities; beauty that is responsible, sustainable, and natural, based on the new green sciences that our laboratories are inventing; and finally, beauty that is diverse and inclusive, adapted to everyone's needs and expectations.

Mirroring this beauty of the future, L'Oréal's new collective adventure will be to invent the company of the future, in the decade 2020–2030:

- A company that is ever more tech and digital—intelligent, agile, connected—where cloud, data, and artificial intelligence will be at the service of "augmented" employees and consumers.
- An exemplary company in terms of responsibility and sustainability, motivated by the new L'Oréal for the Future commitments we made this year.
- And finally, a company where, more than ever, people remain at the heart of everything, and where values, ethics, inclusivity, diversity, development, social protection, and human rights will remain absolute priorities.

Jean-Paul Agon
L'Oréal CEO

Introduction: Building a Beauty Powerhouse

Early in 2010, L'Oréal CEO Jean-Paul Agon, a company lifer with a friendly, easygoing disposition, began experiencing a feeling of premonition, one that had become familiar to him throughout his executive career. Experience told him he should trust this sense that something dramatic was about to take place and that he needed to get ahead of it. Bits of ideas gleaned in informal chats with well-informed friends and in his travels, meeting other leaders, economists, politicians, academics, and media types, were starting to create a picture in his mind of something big that was about to change the course of industry.

In a matter of just a few weeks, the image sharpened: a wave of digital technology that had already transformed many aspects of daily life and business was about to surge with such disruptive intensity that it would transform entire industries and threaten the survival of companies that did not ready themselves in time for its assault. Agon was the night watchman who could sound the alarm. He knew that the future of his century-old company was at stake, and he needed to inspire his colleagues to take action and drive the transformation before the wave overwhelmed them. A charismatic CEO with a sterling record, Agon knew he could count on his senior leadership team to listen and respond. He was far from clear on the actions they should take, but the alarm needed sounding, loud and commanding, now.

To stir his troops to action, Agon resorted to a jarring and violent metaphor. He began predicting the arrival of a digital tsunami. First internally, to his executive committee, then more publicly, he took to forecasting that the relatively peaceful waters of the cosmetics industry were about to be dramatically agitated by a massive tidal wave. He referred to the digital disruption that had begun to shake many sectors and industries, turning market leaders into insignificant players and small entrants into powerhouses overnight. The disruption was about to hit the tranquil shores of the beauty sector, a $500-billion global industry that had, until then, remained relatively unscathed, dominated as it was by a handful of long-established and successful multinational players—Europeans such as L'Oréal and Unilever, Americans such as Procter & Gamble and Estée Lauder, and the Japanese Shiseido.

Most executives, including Agon, had seen the initial technological wave unfurl over the course of their careers: firms had integrated information technology into their operations and were communicating effectively with consumers who used the internet in their daily lives for everything from obtaining information about products they wanted to buy to sending e-mails and posting pictures on social networks. What many businesses across sectors, including cosmetics manufacturers, had failed to recognize was that this first wave had triggered a much more powerful cataclysm that would encompass far more than technology and would in fact transform everything from consumer behavior to the way companies are managed and even which companies would survive. Agon's premonition was right on the mark, auguring a deep and broad upheaval in the sector. He succeeded in rallying his troops to launch L'Oréal's response to the disruption, a dramatic transformation that allowed the company to position itself ahead of the incoming wave.

It is this roughly ten-year transformation that *Digital Makeover: How L'Oréal Put People First to Build a Beauty Tech Powerhouse* explores. Our investigation dives into the breadth and the depth of the disruptive wave, looking not only at the companies and brands that produce beauty products but beyond them, to the way the disruption engulfs consumers of beauty products; influencers such as celebrities, actors, models, journalists, and other opinion leaders whose conversations fuel the demand for these products; value chain partners both upstream and downstream; and, finally, the very core notion of beauty in the minds, practices, and looks of consumers around the world.

The disruption caused by information and digital technology over the course of the past forty years has been broad and multidimensional. Its business dimensions, while enormous, are but one aspect of the overall phenomenon: the deeper sociological, political, and economic ramifications are immense and still being played out at the global, regional, and national levels. The full scope of the disruptive potential was identified and understood early by the most focused and astute observers, many of whom used this advance knowledge very legitimately to build or transform businesses and diffuse generally useful information. Others, having devised less benevolent uses of digital information and digital channels, whether for political or economic reasons, have contributed to the destabilization of the post–Cold War world order. The ability to use digital channels to spread disinformation and further political agendas is an important factor in the rise of populism and poses a significant threat to democracy. The remarkable effectiveness of positive as well as nefarious applications serves to emphasize and remind us of the potential disruptive power of digital technologies.

From Disruption to Transformative Action

The very notion of a market has been disrupted by the availability of information and the disintermediation of many transactions. This has reversed the traditional power dynamics between sellers and buyers. To take the familiar case of consumer goods, consumers now have much more control over their relationship with brands and their purchasing process as they benefit from far greater access to information about the brands and products they select. At the level of individual firms, the incoming wave has been tackled in very different ways. Some leaders, Agon among them, sensed the wave's early signals, understood the power of the disruption as well as the opportunities and challenges it carried with it, and responded by launching a corporate digital transformation early on. Others were less heedful. The retail sector has been particularly disrupted and provides countless examples of bankrupt brands whose failed attempts at transformation were too late or too cautious. Across sectors and companies, disruption remains a survival challenge.

At the personal level, digital disruption has been just as real, and many of us have had to engineer our own digital transformations, in either our professional lives or our personal lives. Take our own digital disruption. We are both business school professors with decades of teaching experience. As educators, we have had to gradually rethink the way we teach. Twenty years ago, we adopted PowerPoint slides as a teaching support. Later, as it became clear that much of the content we had been teaching was readily accessible online, we refocused on guiding students to develop skills and mindsets rather than on delivering content.

More recently, we allowed our students to use devices in class for notetaking and to check out brands, people, and concepts during lectures. We welcomed our students' ability to tap into unlimited amounts of information and data about brands and their strategies, allowing them to benchmark, compare, contrast, and learn. Class presentations grew more elaborate as students mixed media resources creatively and deftly. Gradually, we reimagined our teaching role in the face of changing technology and in response to our students' increased expectations and proactivity. Try competing with a world-renowned, TED-powered expert on a topic you thought you knew inside out!

Then, in March 2020, within the span of a few days, we found ourselves locked down in our respective homes, each facing the prospect of teaching dozens of hours online on a platform we had never used before. Sitting in front of a live webcam for a three-hour lecture was simply not an option. We reinvented our teaching overnight. Steeped in the tradition of business school case studies, we were both adept at leading class discussions. We reimagined our teaching as facilitating virtual collaborative learning, and our role as coaching learning teams. After sharing a few fundamental concepts and frameworks with a class, we sent them into breakout groups at the push of a button to work collaboratively. We rotated virtually among groups, listening in on their conversations, challenging them to dig deeper, and prodding them to take away new learnings and share them with others.

Our relationship with our students grew stronger and became more supportive, more empowering. The feeling was exhilarating, the feedback was enthusiastic, and the possibilities now seem endless. Our digital transformation started gradually and accelerated suddenly. Along the way, we learned that adopting new technologies is decidedly not what digital transformation is about. We and many colleagues have reinvented our role as educators, along with our practices and the very definitions of teaching and learning.

Beauty Disrupted

Together with the travel and hospitality industries, beauty has been one of the sectors most severely affected by the COVID-19 pandemic. The spread of the virus triggered both the closing of retail stores, which most beauty consumers still favored, and the at-home lockdown of the entire population of many countries, drastically decreasing the consumption of many categories of beauty products. The sector has traditionally shown resilience to crisis, often benefiting from the so-called lipstick effect,[1] the documented increase in sales of relatively affordable "feel good" indulgences such as lipstick in periods of crisis. The COVID-19 crisis may force a renaming of this effect to highlight mascara or eye shadow as mask-wearing consumers shift their indulgence buying from lipsticks to eye makeup.

Indeed, what the crisis has precipitated is a shift in the categories consumers look for, as well as in the buying habits of consumers. Self-care categories including luxury soaps, scented candles, aromatherapy, and detox products have experienced renewed vigor. There has also been a notable move away from professional services and toward at-home use of hair coloring and nail-care products. And, of course, online sales have skyrocketed while retail sales vanished overnight.

In a climate of heightened uncertainty, what matters is a company's ability to move fast, to redeploy resources, to shift production from one category to another and/or from one country to another, to find ways to reach out to its customers, to look after its employees, and to keep its eyes focused on both the very short term and the longer term. What these different moves have in common, aside from the fact that they cost money, is that they require the ability to collect, treat, and interpret data, and to ensure that data is looped into strategic decision-making in real time. In other words, beyond deep pockets, it is primarily the ability to manage accelerated cycles of measuring, analyzing, and acting that will make a difference between survival and untimely demise. While no company in the beauty industry will emerge unscathed from the COVID-19 crisis—or any other emergency—the odds are in favor of large, deep-pocketed multinationals with a broad category portfolio who can weather the crisis better than smaller players, allowing sales in one category or one market to compensate for declines in others.

For L'Oréal, the Chinese market began experiencing a resurgence just as the rest of the world was slowing down, resulting in a more distributed impact on resources and cashflow than might be the case for a more local or regional player. On the other hand, companies lacking digital capabilities were hit hard and lost ground. Direct access to consumers via sophisticated e-commerce platforms has allowed some brands to pivot their business in a matter of days from brick-and-mortar retail to online sales. Brands with insufficient capabilities, or without any direct-to-consumer access, could not adapt as fast and lost out. The COVID-19 crisis has served as a powerful reminder of the momentum of the digital disruption wave, and put pressure on many companies to redouble their transformation efforts. We will refer to this digital acceleration effect of the pandemic throughout the book.

The COVID-19 crisis has accelerated not just digital transformation itself, but also the gap between digitally advanced companies and digital laggards. Analysts had previously spoken of an arms race effect in digital transformation. As transformed companies extract more value from digital, and in particular from data, they reinvest in improving their digital capabilities and resources, resulting in an acceleration of performance that leaves those unable to enter into the same cycle further and further behind.

A Human Approach to Digital Transformation

L'Oréal CEO Jean-Paul Agon has called the past ten years the most fascinating time in his forty-year career at L'Oréal. That is quite a statement from a company man who worked his way up from sales to marketing, to larger and larger brands and territories, to the top job in 2006. Beyond telling a fascinating insider's story, our goal in this book is to clarify what digital transformation is and is not. We seek to cast light on digital transformation as a challenging but thoroughly exciting process, underscoring particularly the opportunities it offers to fulfill human needs and encourage more productive human relationships.

We define digital transformation as the digitally enabled deep overhaul of all value-creating relationships, practices, and processes within an ecosystem. In other words, we see the technological dimension of digital transformation merely as an enabler, while it is the human and social dimension that holds the true potential for greater relevance, benefits, and value. In our work with senior executives and leaders, we witness firsthand the anxieties digital disruption brings with it. We believe that what often stands in the way of effective digital transformation is a lack of vision and confidence on the part of a firm's leadership team. This constrains the organization's ambition and chances of success.

Both of us work with executives in the course of our consulting and coaching engagements, and in the executive development programs in which we teach. We remind them of the huge potential of digital technology to improve people's lives and create more relevance for their employees, their customers, their partners, and, more broadly, their ecosystem. By shifting the focus away from technology toward the human, we convince leaders that the seemingly insurmountable first steps of digital transformation are much less daunting and much more familiar than meets the eye. All these first steps require is a simple mind-set shift, which we illustrate with an analogy to surfing. Jay diMartino, a writer and former surfer, suggests that "the simple act of surfing takes less skill than it does desire."[2] We ask our clients: Do you really want to make this transformation happen? Is this your burning desire? If so, get ready to hang ten and make things happen. Let's ride that wave!

DiMartino goes on to talk about a surfer's skills: flexibility, balance, and endurance. Aside from the flexibility needed to adapt your stance to the size and shape of the wave you are tackling, your inner surfer dude will want to practice balance. Digital transformation involves balancing the pull of the future with the grounding of the past. The eight practices of L'Oréal's Simplicity manifesto, which we'll explore in greater detail in Chapter 8, are all about balancing the old and the new: "frame and trust is the new control," "consumer satisfaction is the new product performance." And third, for surfers, is endurance, "pushing through the pain and exhaustion" according to DiMartino. In the coming chapters, we'll show how L'Oréal, like many companies that have survived a century's worth of political crises, financial crashes, and corporate restructurings, has endured its share of pain and exhaustion and come out the other side equipped with resilience.

A Sprightly Grande Dame

Our choice of L'Oréal—a leader in beauty, a profoundly human sector—is not a random one. Beauty is about intimacy, understanding, love, passion, and excitement, not algorithms and A/B testing. Yet, as noted by Agon, there is a natural compatibility between beauty and digital.[3] Beauty-related products and topics rank among those most highly searched on the internet, and beauty is both deeply personal and thoroughly social. Social media has enabled burgeoning beauty-related conversations and interactions among consumers around the world and has served to amplify the social and cultural dimensions of beauty. The beauty sector provides a particularly compelling and illustrative context for us to demonstrate that digital transformation can be led successfully in any industry as a human process, one in which technology is used in service of, not as the driver of, the transformative process.

Another important reason for choosing L'Oréal as a case study is its history, legacy, and age. L'Oréal calls itself one hundred years young. It is a company with a great legacy but one that has had to reinvent itself drastically over the years. The story we tell reveals how a venerable, centenary grande dame turned itself into a young, sprightly ingenue, and highlights all the steps she took to accomplish her makeover. Throughout the book, we will show how key aspects of L'Oréal's culture have contributed to the success of the digital transformation process.

L'Oréal's story begins in 1907, when young Eugène Schueller applied for a patent to manufacture hair dyes. Schueller was the son of hard-working Alsatian parents of modest origin who moved to Paris in 1870 when Alsace fell under German rule. Having inherited his parents' industriousness, Schueller graduated valedictorian in 1904 from France's top chemical engineering school, after putting himself through his studies by working at night.

As Schueller was launching his career in chemistry, he began spending many after-work hours developing hair dyes. After receiving his first patent, he transformed his one-bedroom apartment into a laboratory, where he devoted his nights to inventing formulas that he sold to hairdressers by day. What distinguished Schueller's products from others on the market was the rigorous research behind them. While hair dyes were widely available to French women in those days, many were poorly made and caused dangerous side effects such as burns, rashes, or hair loss. In 1909, having impressed a financier, Schueller founded La Société Française des Teintures Inoffensives pour Cheveux (the French Company for Harmless Hair Dyes), which would eventually become L'Oréal.

The name L'Oréal derived from *l'auréole,* the French word for "halo," a puffed hairstyle that was popular before World War I. To create the halo effect, stylists used hairpieces that were dyed to match a woman's natural hair color. L'Auréale, the brand name under which Schueller's first dyes were marketed, would later inspire the company's current name.

The era immediately preceding World War I was one of scientific and technological innovation in Europe, particularly in France. The political economist Joseph Schumpeter later wrote that entrepreneurs of the time "were to reform or revolutionize the routine of production by exploiting an invention or, more generally, an unprecedented technical possibility."[4] From cars to bicycles, from printing presses to publishing, from cinema to aviation, the French successes of that time reflect tremendous dynamism and rapid growth. On the demand side, consumers across the socioeconomic spectrum were all looking for novelty. Women who experimented with hair products also rode bicycles to claim and proclaim their independence. Schueller's hair dyes reflect the same spirit of optimism and inventiveness, not unlike the start-ups of our time.

Over the following decades, L'Oréal would innovate, invent, and reinvent new products and product lines beyond hair dyes, but the company would also transform itself repeatedly as it developed into a full-fledged beauty conglomerate. In 1918, Schueller expanded into body care by buying the Société des Savons Français, a fledgling soap business, and later diversified into shampoo and sun care. Ambre Solaire was created in 1936, the year the socialist Front Populaire government gave all French workers the right to annual paid leave. It was the end of the cult of fair skin, and a golden tan became a symbol of empowerment and return to nature.

Le Grand L'Oréal

Schueller carefully selected his successor, François Dalle. He had put Dalle at the head of the soap business at the onset of World War II, when Dalle was just twenty-three. The two men worked alongside each other for many years until Schueller designated Dalle as CEO in 1957. Schueller correctly saw that Dalle had what it took to turn L'Oréal into a large, well-structured international firm, what he called "Le Grand L'Oréal." Dalle would remain CEO for twenty-seven years, during which L'Oréal flourished and conquered the world.

Dalle sensed a trend in lifestyle and consumer desires toward more body hygiene, and he invested in body care, including deodorants, bath products, and moisturizers. In 1965, he expanded into skin care and luxury with the acquisition of Lancôme. More brands followed, both through acquisitions and in-house development.

On the distribution side, Dalle maintained close relationships with leading retailers and developed a critical presence in the drug and pharmaceutical sectors. His investment in the pharmaceutical sector increased L'Oréal's capabilities and legitimacy in research and development, a function that grew dramatically in the Dalle years, ramping up from twenty researchers at the end of World War II to fifteen hundred at the time of his retirement.

International development played a big role in Dalle's conquest strategy to build Le Grand L'Oréal. It was conducted in a systematic, rigorous, and sometimes militaristic way, with a number of homegrown rules of engagement, including his beloved "breach theory," an all-out effort to attain an unassailable beachhead position in a given market. Dalle also assembled a small cadre of young business pioneers who were willing to move to new markets and embed themselves to soak up local intelligence, implement company strategies, and deliver on aggressive targets.

Markets were selected following a concentric circle pattern, starting with familiar ones where cultural differences were few and expanding progressively toward farther-flung territories such as Latin America, Africa, and Asia as the company's knowledge of international practices and customs grew. The exception to the concentric strategy was Japan, an early favorite market of Dalle's.

Dalle also went about modeling the company's organizational structure and processes on his American competitors, particularly Procter & Gamble, which he admired greatly. He was an early adopter of just-in-time manufacturing techniques and imported efficiency techniques. He created corporate-level staff functions and divisions around the different distribution channels: Consumer Products to target mass-market consumers, L'Oréal Professional for hair professionals, Active Beauty for pharmacies, and Perfumes and Beauty for luxury and specialty retailers. And finally, he brought in IBM to develop the company's technological backbone.

Perhaps the most crucial aspect of Dalle's legacy is the deal he struck with Nestlé in 1973. By investing in L'Oréal, the Swiss food and beverage giant provided significant capital for growth while protecting L'Oréal from foreign acquisition as well as from potential takeover by an eventual socialist government. It has provided L'Oréal the breathing space and security the company needed to continue its expansion at a critical time in its history. The deal was encouraged and endorsed by then–French president Georges Pompidou, who was eager to guarantee the autonomy of an emblematic leader of French industry.

Consolidating Leadership

The Dalle conquest years were followed by another period of great ambition and achievement led by Welsh-born Lindsay Owen-Jones, who served from 1988 to 2006 as CEO (and until 2011 as chairman).

The Owen-Jones era can best be summed up as one of globalization and leadership for L'Oréal. The company consolidated its position and turned these achievements into an enviable worldwide leadership position. Under Owen-Jones, the international strategy shifted from conquest to a highly effective acquisition and development war machine that combined insightful market knowledge and an incontrovertible expertise in strategic brand management.

When Jean-Paul Agon stepped into the CEO role in 2006, he inherited a world leader in beauty with a diversified but focused portfolio of brands and products, and a strong position across continents. He was poised for a different kind of strategy, one whose objective is to strengthen the company's ability to withstand a more uncertain and volatile environment. The Owen-Jones war machine had to give way to a newer kind of offensive weaponry, one built on agility, adaptability, diversity, and innovation.

This is where Jean-Paul Agon stood in 2010, four years into his CEO role, when he sounded the digital tsunami warning and declared 2010 the Digital Year. He urged his leadership team to dig deep into the core identity of the company and to think about reinventing not just L'Oréal but beauty itself. Agon admits candidly that the road ahead was far from obvious to him at that point. In fact, his ability to mobilize his colleagues so fervently behind this digital reinvention is that much more impressive considering his confession that he lacked a clear sense of where it would land them. For four years, Agon led the makeover from the top. He knew that he would soon need to bring in an expert to craft a coherent plan and lead L'Oréal into its implementation, but he had to wait for the right person at the right time.

In 2014, Agon appointed Lubomira Rochet to the position of Chief Digital Officer, giving the thirty-six-year-old beauty neophyte a seat on the corporate Executive Committee, together with a clear and straightforward brief to establish and implement a roadmap for the digital transformation of L'Oréal. Rochet has since become the architect, the strategist, the champion, and the face of L'Oréal's digital transformation, bringing passion, talent, and vision to the role.

In June 2020, Agon declared his intention to retire in the spring of 2021. Just four months later, in October, L'Oréal announced that Nicolas Hiéronimus, deputy CEO in charge of divisions, would become L'Oréal's next CEO upon Agon's retirement. Following the company's well-established tradition, Hiéronimus is a L'Oréal insider who has spent his entire career at the company, starting in 1987 on the Garnier brand as product manager and later marketing director, and rising remarkably swiftly to serve as general manager for L'Oréal Paris, and president of the Luxe division before heading up all divisions. Like most L'Oréal executives groomed for senior leadership roles, Hiéronimus was given international operational exposure along the way, first as general manager for Maybelline and Garnier in the United Kingdom, and later as general manager of L'Oréal Mexico for three years.

In a break with tradition, the appointment of a new deputy CEO was announced simultaneously. That role goes to Barbara Lavernos, current Chief Technology Officer, also a L'Oréal lifer. The choice of Lavernos and the timing of her promotion make clear L'Oréal's commitment to promoting greater opportunities for women (some had hoped for a woman CEO), as well as the critical role that technology will play in the years to come. Hiéronimus himself is known as a strong advocate of the core role of technology in the company's strategy and future strategy. No clearer message of L'Oréal's beauty tech positioning could have been given than the announcement of the Hiéronimus/Lavernos duo. Together, they inherit a $30 billion business with thirty-six global brands and a presence in 150 markets, and will lead a workforce of 86,000 employees throughout the world. Agon will hand over a company whose deep transformation has left no unit, no process, no function, no practice unchanged. In the last year of his leadership, Agon will have led L'Oréal through the COVID-19 crisis, a successful stress test of sorts for his legacy as the initiator and orchestrator of the digital transformation.

Inspiring Digital Transformation

The last few pages notwithstanding, our perspective in this book is not that of historians but of management experts. We go beyond documenting and uncovering how the transformation unfolded to analyze what has made it successful. Our aim is to define an approach to digital transformation that can inspire executives in other sectors.

Before analyzing the different aspects of the transformation, we take an in-depth look at the cultural history of the more than one-hundred-year-old company. In Part I, we identify four foundational cultural pillars, the origins of which can be traced back to the early years of the company: orchestrate creativity, cultivate healthy doubt, learn and innovate with rigor, and listen with curiosity. These pillars have been reinforced over the years, fashioned along the way by the style of each of the five CEOs and by the internal and external challenges that make up the reality of a thriving multinational business. The pillars are just as fundamental to the legacy of L'Oréal as they are relevant to today's digital challenges and provide a useful lesson in balancing the old and the new. They define the way the company is run; how L'Oréal managers make decisions; how they recruit people and develop talent; how they conduct meetings, enter markets, manage competition, develop products, and bring them to market; and more.

The principles behind the four pillars are well known and commonly articulated within L'Oréal, a sign that they are deeply engrained in the culture. For a company whose main structural attribute is its decentralization, the pillars provide the support and the framework that allow the thirty-six brands and 150 country units to function as a coherent whole. Part I leaves us with a clear understanding that a culturally entrenched mindset that combines orchestrated creativity, healthy doubt, rigorous testing and learning, and constant curiosity has served the company well by helping it adapt to vastly changing contexts over its history.

L'Oréal's decentralized structure has also favored a combined top-down and bottom-up approach during much of the company's history, enabling the creative ideas that naturally emerge from a diversity of markets and contexts to rise up to the corporate level, while strong leadership and a reassuring sense of direction are constantly reinforced from the top. The result, described by some, including Agon, as organized chaos, can hardly be faulted on the basis of performance. These conclusions point to a critical factor of L'Oréal's success over its history—it is all about its people and how they work together. There is a comfort in this conclusion that a company whose business is human beauty and well-being succeeds in large part as a result of its focus on people.

Part II is a deep dive into the core of the digital makeover along the human and social dimensions of its complex ecosystem. We show how L'Oréal has managed the transformation of its ecosystem, focusing in turn on its relationship with consumers, the relationships among consumers and with influencers, and its partnerships with its upstream and downstream partners. In our final chapter, we delve into the cultural transformation that L'Oréal's leadership team has orchestrated alongside and as a complement to the digital transformation.

At the end of each chapter, we offer "transformation tips," a summary of the takeaway points that are particularly useful in leading a digital transformation. Most of them are very practical and provide a strong basis for the elaboration and implementation of your own digital transformation strategy. While many of our readers will be familiar with L'Oréal and its brands, we provide appendices containing useful background information in the form of a timeline documenting key moments in the company's history, a list of L'Oréal brands and when they were launched or joined the company, and some industry data for comparison. We have also included pictures to illustrate some of the anecdotes we relate in the book.

In writing *Digital Makeover*, we aim to provide a highly informative, thought-provoking, approachable, and entertaining read that inspires you to approach digital transformation with greater confidence and by putting people first. Whether you are leading a digital transformation, looking to better understand how digital transformations are carried out, or simply curious about L'Oréal and the beauty industry, join us for the ride. And if you don't know your K-beauty from your indies, your DTC from your programmatic, or your conversion rates from your livestreaming, we've got some answers for you!

DIGITAL MAKEOVER

Four Foundational Pillars

High on the list of digital disruptions experienced by established beauty companies is the appearance and success in the market of newer and distinctive "indie" brands, many launched by celebrities and other influencers with direct-to-consumer (DTC) access. Some benefit from a founder's following (Kylie Jenner's Kylie Cosmetics, Rihanna's Fenty, Kim Kardashian's KKW), a specific target (teenagers, women with problem skin, Black professional women), or a particular type of products (plant-based skin care, clean beauty) and often elicit passion from their communities of customers.

The DTC model is efficient and promotes a high-touch, intimate, and trusting relationship with customers that is conducive to strong loyalty. One of these brands, Glossier, originally built up as a beauty blog, is now a successful brand of "natural look" products sold to its huge and passionate community of followers. Indie brands have eaten into the market share of established legacy brands in recent years, ranking high on the "what keeps me up at night" list of many legacy company executives.

L'Oréal has successfully maintained its dominance in the face of the indie challenge. Besides its deeper pockets, the magnitude of the data its brands can access, share, and exploit, the reputation of its brands, and the scale of many other resources, L'Oréal benefits from an accumulation of decades of experience, expertise, knowledge, and culture. These intangible assets have enabled its brands to reimagine their business models by nurturing new markets, testing out new products, taking calculated risks, learning on the fly, and generally taking a more patient long-term perspective than the newer players can afford to.

In this first part of the book, we will focus specifically on how instrumental L'Oréal's rich cultural legacy has been to its digital transformation and ability to withstand the indie challenge. Although it represents only one aspect of digital disruption, the indie phenomenon underlines how digital technology has transformed the way humans relate to one another, and has created opportunities for new, more relevant social interactions and relationships. L'Oréal's more than one hundred years of experience and accumulation of time-tested cultural practices have served it particularly well in this context.

We will focus on four pillars, which our thorough analysis and experience of L'Oréal's culture have helped us identify: orchestrate creativity, cultivate healthy doubt, learn and innovate with rigor, and listen with curiosity. We call these four elements *pillars* because they constitute the foundation of L'Oréal's culture and account in great part for its fortitude. Far from being immutable, these pillars owe their robustness to the way they have developed and risen as a result of changing contexts and leadership styles. It is, again, this balancing act between deep loyalty to the past and a healthy desire for innovation that has made L'Oréal's culture and its pillars highly adaptive and made it so successful in the face of digital disruption. We now look deep into the company's history to uncover these pillars as they have been fashioned by the women and men of L'Oréal through their day-to-day work and practices over the past ten decades.

ORCHESTRATE CREATIVITY

Mention digital transformation and you conjure up ideas about e-commerce, social networks, and big data. Too often, we overlook the fact that it is also about the strategic and organizational processes within the company itself. Digital transformation brings with it profound organizational change, a change that relies on and impacts individuals deep in the ranks of the company yet requires coordination by a strong leader.

At L'Oréal, CEO Jean-Paul Agon initiated and orchestrated the transformation by preaching relentlessly for change and by drawing from the company's legacy and culture to activate the transformation. L'Oréal has a long tradition of balancing creativity and inspiration with discipline and scientific rigor, whether it be in its dual-channel approach to research or its distinctive market-entry strategies. When encouraged to emanate from deep within the organization, creativity delivers innovative solutions that are truly relevant and responsive to the market. Scientific discipline and rigor can boost the impact of disparate solutions from across the organization by turning them into explicit knowledge to be shared throughout the organization.

For Agon—faced with a double objective of bringing the entire organization on board and transforming it through and through—the tried-and-true blend of creativity and rigor offered a natural path forward. Although the need for a profound transformation seems obvious in retrospect, the 2010 context in which Agon declared a digital emergency was very different from our current understanding of the business landscape. Having had the vision and confidence to declare a digital emergency, Agon not only needed to get buy-in throughout, he also had to think ahead to how he would operationalize the transformation more broadly. In resolving this dilemma, Agon's priority course of action combined a strong and urgent message from the top with an invitation to the entire organization to innovate and improvise.

Enabling improvisation is an important way for a leader to blend creativity and discipline. Jazz music is legendary for its reliance on improvisation, as illustrated by the story of trumpet player and bandleader Miles Davis's recording session for his 1959 album, *Kind of Blue*. Davis showed up at the recording studio with two new musical modes that had never been played before. With no time to reflect on how to use these modes, band members had to improvise by integrating them into the performance at the same time they discovered the modes: they combined the creativity of adapting the forms to their own style and mood with the rigor of sticking to the required forms. *Kind of Blue* turned out to be one of the greatest jazz recordings of all time. No time to ask questions—just discover, dive in, and improvise. Agon's digital emergency declaration was nothing short of the proclamation of a new type of musical harmony for L'Oréal. While the score was being written, he demanded that the entire organization face up to this new beat and let it guide and inspire future initiatives. These improvised responses, tentative and disparate at first, would eventually be harmonized and made to rise into a full-blown collective achievement: creativity integrated with discipline.

Having inspired improvisation, Agon launched the second phase of L'Oréal's digital transformation by appointing a CDO. There was still plenty of room for improvisation but, little by little, improvised practices were formalized and shared across units and supported by the new leader as cohesion, harmony, and systematicity traveled from the parts to the whole. Throughout the process, Agon held on to his evangelist role by consistently delivering the same urgent and reassuring message: digital is our collective imperative; it starts with you, but it belongs to all of us.

The Importance of an Evangelist

Digital transformation is first and foremost a change process. And, as with any significant change, it requires strong leadership and determination if it is to succeed. This simple statement does not, however, capture the true complexity of transformation. And this is particularly true for a digital makeover, where everything ranging from new products to new partnerships, new manufacturing processes to new supply chains, new practices to new functions and business units has to be rethought from scratch. It must all be reimagined and reinvented, often in real time, and in a context of great uncertainty, volatility, and, very often, anxiety throughout the company.

From the start of his digital mission, Agon was driven by his profound belief that the moment for transformation had come and that any delay would severely jeopardize the future of the company. Having decreed 2010 "the digital year," he embarked on a crusade to convince L'Oréal's employees that digital transformation was no longer optional, a message he reinforced consistently and vehemently over time. In true L'Oréal fashion, much of Agon's conviction came from his observations and discussions with leaders across sectors and his thorough understanding of the sector and the market. He notes, "Some friends in the digital world were explaining what was going on, and I realized a tsunami was coming. I could see it from far away."[1] Throughout the history of L'Oréal, the CEO's personal conviction provided the impetus for major changes; that conviction has often developed organically through personal experience, sometimes serendipitously, other times more systematically.

Among L'Oréal's direct competitors, French cosmetics house Clarins had already begun to make significant strides in digital transformation. On the retail side, Sephora was developing innovative approaches, particularly in the United States, built on data collection using its loyalty programs and e-commerce platforms. While L'Oréal's direct big competitors were increasingly investing in digital media and distribution, none of them had undergone a wholesale digital transformation. Similarly, digital had yet to accelerate the beauty sector's massive shift toward the ascent of indie brands, often led by highly influential celebrities. Agon's crusade was motivated by his faith in the power of digital, but it also reflected his recognition that there were no simple rules of the game for how to go about orchestrating a digital transformation. There was no roadmap and Agon wasn't about to pretend to have one.

One thing Agon understood from the very beginning is that digital transformation, more than any previous type of change initiative, must involve the entire organization and, beyond that, the whole system around it, including its customers and partners such as distributors, retailers, and others. Not only does digital transformation foster greater participation within the entire system, but it can only happen through a participative process, a lesson that brands learned the hard way early on when they tried to censor customer reviews or critics. In 2010, having been accused by Greenpeace of using unsustainable palm oil in its KitKat bars, Nestlé tried to silence the critics by claiming their video, which had gone viral, broke copyright laws. The social media uproar was such that the company had to reverse course. It learned that the power of consumers could not simply be ignored and instead had to be used as an opportunity to better understand and respond to their needs. Nestlé eventually learned to engage with its critics and the wider market, and used the opportunity to overhaul its product sourcing and policies.[2] The very nature of digital technology is that it allows information to circulate freely and to be shareable. Once let loose, information is there to be used by anyone who has access to it and is able to, or chooses to, participate. This is true for customers who share product reviews and how-to tips, as well as for employees whose success stories through trial and error are extolled as best practices.

Agon recognized the value of sharing information to promote participation, as well as the value of participation in the transformation process. He wanted digital transformation to touch all areas of the company and to involve everyone. The process, in his view, demanded an open mind and a relentless desire to experiment. This is the message he repeated every time he spoke, both within and outside the company—he never visited a division or country without addressing the issue of digital transformation and encouraging participation and experimentation. In 2011, for the first time, L'Oréal devoted a chapter of its annual report to digital projects, a move that symbolized the tenacity of Agon and his board of directors in pursuing the digital endeavor as participative.

Across the company, executives began to embark on a series of digital initiatives, many of which were true improvisations. Agon heartily encouraged and supported all of the experiments, even the most imaginative, from taking a chance with up-and-coming influencers to querying search data for creative product development to inventing new ways for hair colorists to better serve their clients.

Time to Improvise

As in many other companies, the early days of digital transformation caused confusion and anxiety. Markets such as the United States took an early lead in integrating digital initiatives around customers' path to purchase.[3] In a 2011 interview, then U.S. Chief Marketing Officer Mark Speichert was sanguine about the strategic opportunities not just in increasing digital spending and building partnerships with digital players, but more generally in rethinking the relationship between brands and consumers.

On the other hand, at the corporate level, the 2010 annual report was more cautious in addressing the scale of the transformation to come, seeking to "secure L'Oréal's leadership in the digital channel."[4] Reflected here is the fact that many understood the need to use digital tools to communicate both internally and externally but didn't appreciate the magnitude of the technological, societal, and human changes that were about to unfold. L'Oréal's areas of great strength and competence had always been its impressive product development capabilities and its intimate understanding of distribution channels in all its markets. In spite of Agon's reassurances, digital reared its head as an unknown and somewhat ominous development for many: suddenly, the tried-and-true formulas of success, no matter how much innovation they had delivered, were no longer enough. Not only was the mold broken, it had to be thrown out the window and who knew if another one would ever replace it? Because the company did not have its own retail network, it did not have much direct access to consumers other than through retail brands such as Kiehl's and The Body Shop, companies it had acquired in 2000 and 2006, respectively.[5]

The new digital focus laid bare the lack of direct interactions between L'Oréal and its customers and the massive challenge this presents for a company trying to turn itself from its traditional focus on product to consumer centricity. Digital technology has made consumer centricity an imperative for consumer-facing and industrial companies across sectors. Often misunderstood as renewed focus on customer service, consumer centricity is a profound strategic, operational, and cultural shift for organizations. As consumers have gained greater control over how they choose, buy, and experience products and services thanks to digital technology, they have become much more demanding of the brands they select. At the same time, companies can access so much information about consumers that they can develop products, services, and, more generally, experiences that are much more relevant to individual and small segments of their customers than ever before. Consumer centricity does, however, require the ability to collect data directly from consumers, something that is difficult for brands that do

not have direct-to-consumer access via retail operations or digital platforms, and poses significant privacy and ethical challenges.

Inside the organization, the realization that the digital initiative was
much more than the introduction of some digital tools and that it would
lead to wholesale transformation in the way the company did business
challenged people's thinking of what made L'Oréal a dominant player.
For most of its history, hard scientific research and innovation were
such a strong core competence for L'Oréal that it even ventured into
the pharmaceutical sector. It had also built an impregnable distribution
network throughout the world, based on a strategic approach to sales,
painstaking on-the-ground sales efforts across its markets near and far,
and, in large part, unequaled market research. In many ways, these two
elements of L'Oréal's success—outstanding research and distribution—
now made it ill-prepared for consumer centricity. Scientifically informed
product development is exactly that, and it is not easily compatible with
consumer-informed innovation. Close partnerships with distributors
and retailers often require that a company steer clear of the direct-to-
consumer relationships that are crucial to a consumer-centric strategy.

The task of transforming L'Oréal toward consumer centricity was
immense. And, while Agon's vision was strong, to believe that L'Oréal's
digital transformation was driven by a firm idea of where it would
eventually lead would be to seriously misunderstand the process the
company went through. In fact, his strong vision was coupled with a calculated creative blurriness that left lots of room for local brand leaders to
innovate with and for their own customers. This blurriness is precisely
why Agon's approach of letting people up and down the organization
improvise in response to his call to action was so appropriate and effective. What Agon was looking for through this improvisation approach
was twofold: on the one hand, he wanted people to start buying into
the need for and opportunities to be derived from digital transformation and to "get on board"; on the other hand, he was looking for people
throughout the organization to participate and start building some great
digital initiatives that would serve as proofs of concept for the very idea
of digital transformation. The two are clearly related: as more proof of
concept projects emerge, more people come on board, and vice versa.

Agon has referred to this first phase as one of chaos,[6] albeit "organized chaos." The systems scientist Peter Senge calls such a state of
ambiguity "creative tension," a tension that produces intense energy
if channeled properly. Agon himself used the metaphor of a volcano,

saying, "It's a bit hot but it produces a lot of energy." Other management experts have referred to an "aesthetic of forgiveness" that makes experimentation and exploration permissible.[7] What is clear is the highly productive effect of giving up control and accepting uncertainty in the face of the unknown. The poet John Keats referred to this idea as "negative capability." He described it as a quality that William Shakespeare "possessed so enormously . . . that is, when a man is capable of being in uncertainties, mysteries, doubts, without any irritable reaching after fact and reason."[8]

This first improvisational phase of the digital transformation started in 2010 and carried on for a few years without a formal framework and without a leader other than Agon himself. Instead, the global chief marketing officer, Marc Menesguen, was tasked by Agon to "accelerate the movement to strengthen L'Oréal's leadership in digital, intensify initiatives, and develop expertise."[9] At the same time, Georges-Edouard Dias, senior VP for e-business, was charged with deploying some of the new initiatives, particularly in the area of programmatic advertising. The ambiguity and ambivalence between these different roles reflect a real tension between vision and current reality, and between intuition and pragmatism within the organization.

Luxury Leads the Way

At L'Oréal, some of the early digital experiments and successes came from the luxury sector, with Lancôme taking a pioneering role in opening a retail website at the end of the 1990s and developing apps in various countries, including China in 2010. The luxury division as a whole managed to achieve 50 percent of L'Oréal's global turnover in e-commerce in 2013.

Lancôme continued in its pioneering role and ventured into the realm of digital entertainment with the launch of the Hypnôse Doll Eyes mascara in 2011, drawing consumers in with an animated teaser film and an app that allowed them to create their own doll avatar modeled after the film's characters. The film was viewed by more than three million consumers and contributed to making 2011 Lancôme's best year in fifteen years, signaling a real renaissance for a brand that had slowly been losing its youthful luster. Lancôme continued to use social media to rejuvenate its image and build greater engagement with a younger audience by launching its new lipstick Rouge in Love with a video featuring

Emma Watson that went viral, reaching 120 million viewers in China in 2013. In addition to these initiatives, the Luxury Division multiplied and expanded its e-commerce experiences through its Kiehl's brand, which benefits from its own retail channel. The huge risk-taking and creative impetus behind these initiatives is difficult to qualify but is testimony to Agon's success in fostering significant improvisational drive and audacity.

By launching the new L'Oréal Paris Super Liner Blackbuster with an unprecedented integrated digital presence across channels, including search, social, blogs, and YouTube tutorials, the Consumer Products Division also showed that it had received the leader's message loud and clear, and in turn sent a clear strategic message to the market that L'Oréal was now fully committed to digital and would spare no means to build a dominant digital position. Around the same time, the L'Oréal Paris brand also began using insights gained online to fuel product innovation, with the introduction of ombré hair color products. Using a combination of search and social data, the brand identified the ombré consumer trend of blending different shades of the same color over the length of the hair and responded swiftly by launching a new line of products. Thanks to their intimate understanding of what consumers were searching for and talking about, the brand's marketers were able to target consumers more effectively and to build brand awareness quickly and establish ombré as a new high-performance style.

For its part, the Professional Products Division also heeded Agon's call by introducing the Salonworld platform, offering hair professionals advice and training as well as opportunities to connect with their community. In 2012, the Active Cosmetics Division began innovating around omnichannel opportunities by launching eSkin, a successful information and advice platform in China, integrating a loyalty club, apps, retail and online stores, and social networks.

Digital innovation was also brought in from outside the company. In 2012, L'Oréal acquired two American brands that targeted millennials: Urban Decay, an affordable luxury brand, and NYX, a mass-market brand. Both brought L'Oréal much-needed experience in mastering social networks, digital marketing, and multichannel distribution. NYX, in particular, routinely co-developed its products with beauty bloggers. Beyond the competencies they injected into L'Oréal, these acquisitions also provided powerful inspiration for other brands within the L'Oréal group. The group's brand leaders were encouraged to visit NYX headquarters in San Francisco and meet its executives in order to develop ties and learn from their new little sister's digital culture. As a result of these integration efforts, a L'Oréal Paris boutique, launched in Paris in 2016, incorporated many of NYX's trademark digital tools, including in-store tablets with tutorials, screens showing Instagram posts in real time, and a display of top bloggers' favorite products. Shoppers get to take home a video of their own in-store makeup tutorial.

Expect Failure

With experimentation inevitably comes failure. One notable disappointment was the ill-fated partnership with YouTube celebrity Michelle Phan, launched in 2013. The "modern essentials" makeup brand, named Em ("sister" in Vietnamese), was introduced online to great fanfare and with ambitious mass-market aspirations. In 2014, it was featured on Amazon's Luxury Beauty Store but never managed to get past the start-up phase and inspire a critical mass of Phan's young followers; eventually, the line was sold back to Phan. The takeaways were harsh for both Phan and L'Oréal: consumers have minds of their own and expecting a celebrity's YouTube fans to become customers of that celebrity's brand is a big ask, particularly when the brand is owned by a multinational company that operates with its own rules. For Michelle Phan, the brand's failure to connect with her followers marked the start of a profound reflection journey to better understand and formulate the distinctive inspiration she can offer her fans, and for L'Oréal it was a sobering reminder of the power of consumers and fans.

Bring in the Tech

In 2012, L'Oréal created an incubator in San Francisco, dubbed the "CBI" (for Connected Beauty Institute), that housed a diverse team of twenty people dedicated to the search for new services that could be developed and delivered via digital technologies. The most innovative project was Makeup Genius, released in 2013. This virtual makeover app simulates makeup application, allowing consumers to "try on" colors before purchase, using their own image on a webcam or a smartphone photo. Beyond its tremendous commercial success, particularly in the

Chinese market, the app served as a milestone that marked L'Oréal's ability to come out with a powerful statement in the digital space.

The success of Makeup Genius provided highly visible and unquestionable proof that the group could indeed position itself at the cutting edge of digital innovation. Internally, Makeup Genius served to increase confidence and to spawn lots of innovative tech-enabled beauty solutions, ranging from sun exposure sensors to an acne scanner. It also pushed L'Oréal's marketers to begin to think much more strategically about how to use the enormous amounts of data collected through the app.

Where To from Here?

As the different digital initiatives, or proofs of concept, we have just reviewed unfolded one after the other across divisions, they built much more than a collection of successes and failures. They constituted an organic learning process born from improvisation, the desire to participate, the creative impetus to contribute to something bigger than one product or one brand. The improvisation logic was starting to deliver. Failure became somewhat more tolerable, experimentation increased, and people learned from one another and from their mistakes. Employees began to respond to one another's initiatives by taking them further, embellishing and improving along the way. Agon has referred to this phase as one of creative chaos. The aesthetic forgiveness that characterized this first step of the transformation also allowed a shift in human relationships at L'Oréal: openness to one another became prized, and a collective spirit began to take shape.

But critical questions also arose: How could the company scale up the various projects developed by brands or countries? How would it manage different levels of digital maturity across markets and brands? Complicating matters was a disappointing e-commerce performance in 2014; only 3.5 percent of sales were from online purchases that year, less than the market average of 5 percent, a sobering result that prompted L'Oréal to rethink the overall e-commerce strategy and give greater focus to consumers' omnichannel experiences throughout their journey with a brand.

To address these and other emerging challenges and aware of the need to accelerate digital transformation and to create an internal strategic framework, Agon called on French digital consulting firm

Valtech to help him define L'Oréal's digital strategy. Valtech's Managing Director for Southern Europe was a talented young consultant named Lubomira Rochet.

From Creative Chaos to Orchestrated Rigor

In 2014, L'Oréal became the first company on the French stock market CAC 40 to include a chief digital officer on its executive committee, recruiting Lubomira Rochet for the position.

The recruitment of a CDO happened relatively early at L'Oréal, compared with its direct competitors and other consumer goods companies. One of Valtech's chief recommendations was to recruit a digital leader and give them a seat on the executive committee, who would consolidate the nascent digital initiatives and strategies across brands, divisions, and markets, and formulate and implement a digital roadmap. In early 2014, the executive committee approved this recommendation.

The Unlikely CDO

Rochet was selected by the executive committee after an extensive internal and external search revealed that she was by far the most qualified candidate to "orchestrate and channel the flow of energy" that had been unleashed in the improvisation phase.[10] Her four-year experience as a Valtech consultant advising L'Oréal on its digital strategy did not spare her from having to sit through fifteen interviews before she was finally tapped as Chief Digital Officer. Unanimously endorsed by the executive committee, she became the fourth woman and the youngest member on a committee composed essentially of pure "L'Oréalians." This term is typically used for lifers who start in the company early in their careers and who embody its values and culture. Interestingly, for a company whose products are targeted primarily at women, Loréalians were mostly men until recent years.

Successful CDOs cut an unusual profile in many organizations. The position requires a leader who can promote a digital culture but whose perspective goes far beyond technology, someone who can advance digital transformation in the face of resistance and convince others that change is imperative. It calls for a profoundly empathetic approach that turns people throughout the organization into partners, co-creators, and evangelists themselves, and bandleader-type charisma to rouse audiences and bring them into the project. Rochet fit the bill on all counts. And yet, technology was not the path Rochet had initially set for herself. An economist by training, she had intended to pursue a career as a civil servant but became fascinated with Silicon Valley's tech boom and optimistic atmosphere when she spent a year at the University of California at Berkeley in the early 2000s. She was amazed to see that "people were betting millions of dollars on guys in flip-flops."[11]

When Rochet returned to France, she joined the IT consulting company Sogeti, a subsidiary of Capgemini, where she became VP of strategy, specializing in the development of digital and software solutions. She described her early days this way: "I was trained as an economist, not an engineer; I had never written a line of code before. I was scared to death and full of envy. I always tried to go off-center, to go where I can bring something because of my difference."[12] Later, after leading Microsoft's start-up and innovation ecosystem for France, she and a friend took over Valtech, an independent digital agency, where she consulted on digital transformation for clients such as Rolex, Chanel, Louis Vuitton, Michelin, Allianz, Société Générale, and L'Oréal.

Indefatigable Determination

Agon was impressed by Rochet's eclectic background, curiosity, and intelligence.[13] Others pointed out that Rochet exhibits the characteristic strength of immigrants, that of being able to adapt to any environment. She was born in Bulgaria and her family moved first to Morocco when she was five years old, then to Paris when she was thirteen. Among the staunch Loréalians, some first saw her as an intruder while others found her talents overrated. She admits to experiencing more than a few moments of solitude at first and found it difficult to fit in as a woman, particularly as a young woman with no experience of the beauty sector, or of business itself. She responded by throwing herself into her mission to accelerate digital transformation. Her strategy was one of trial and error to learn what worked and what didn't, and of reliance on building relationships.

As a relatively new breed, CDOs don't have too many best practices to draw from: they have to invent everything—their job, their role, their projects, their teams, their working methods, their strategy, their models, their metrics. They have to figure out how to involve the entire company, how to work with the Human Resources department to spread digital culture, how to build on existing projects, and how to create and strengthen digital teams, all while developing digital assets such as e-commerce sites, insight platforms, and more.

Call in the Commandos

Rochet initially formulated two objectives for herself: to define an overall strategy for digital and to create a core group of digital experts whose role it is to enable and support the transformation process across the company. She sees herself and her team as enablers, commandos who can intervene rapidly on specific strike missions and then leave each team to continue to implement their projects on their own, having learned from the digital intervention. Beyond their interventions, the commandos also play a critical role in disseminating ideas and practices as they travel from headquarters to the field and back. Success stories resulting from improvisation turn into practices that are shared across markets. Codification, consistency, and coherence are driven by headquarters but are informed by and adapted to local practices and contextual requirements. Rochet's vision and the change management approach she adopted reflect her desire to transform the company without creating additional silos; to create links between divisions, brands, and countries; and to multiply the human interactions that facilitate the integration of digital into the core of the business.

More concretely, she chose to work with a small core team of twenty experts in different facets of digital strategy who combined so-called hard tech skills and soft people skills; she also relied on a broader network of six hundred digital employees, who had begun working across divisions, brands, and geographical groups. At the heart of Rochet's mission is the desire to enable L'Oréal units to deploy digital tools to reach their customers in the right place; at the right time; with the right messages, products, and experiences; and through the right channels. Borrowing from the language of entrepreneurship, she sees the role of the core digital team as enabling the acceleration and scaling of local projects to give them greater scope, visibility, and impact: "We are here to facilitate, not to make," Rochet repeats constantly.[14] In other words, she will never press her ideas on a business or operational executive, choosing instead to inspire and support them as they implement the digital transformation in ways that make sense for their piece of the business. In her view, a CDO "must have frugal leadership, where what matters is not how many armies you have, but how many disciples."[15]

Establishing the Roadmap

As a first step, Rochet decided to push e-commerce in high-volume markets such as the United States and France, as well as in emerging markets with high digital penetration such as Indonesia and Turkey. For this, she used growth-hacking techniques, setting seemingly impossible targets for ad hoc teams of experts to attain by inventing innovative solutions to reach them. She explained, "E-commerce is, after all, only a retail channel like any other, with banners as gondolas and category management as merchandising."[16]

She set out to demystify digital transformation, using simple words and avoiding acronyms, and convincing local teams to do the same. Her enormous energy and the unfailing support she received from Agon inspired people at all levels of the company to embrace digital and digital transformation. Commenting on Rochet's mission, Agon noted, "You'd have to live in a hermit's cave, not to have seen the upheaval caused by digital technology. . . . Digital transforms relationships with distributors and consumers, but also internally with our teams of employees throughout the organization."[17] Having achieved awareness and buy-in through improvisation, the time was now right to deploy a strategic roadmap that would transform every single aspect of the company, and this is what Rochet was about to do.

Enabling Resonance

Even as the digital transformation strategy was now driven from Paris by Rochet and her core team, it continued to be enabled and supported across markets via decentralized initiatives and experiences. Once a digital process had been tried and put in place, it had to be shared with others via conversations, presentations, and a variety of other interactions so it would resonate with other units, striking an evocative chord and building coherence and consistency across the organization.

This process, which we call resonance, is powerful in allowing corporate digital strategy and local initiatives to evolve in response to each other. Resonance is facilitated in a granular way through daily conversations among people across the organization, from the CDO team to different units and local markets, and through a high level of mobility among executives. While enabling back-and-forth knowledge sharing between local units and headquarters has clearly been taken to a strategic level as part of the digital transformation process, it is hardly new.

Agon himself had experienced such knowledge transfer when, at the age of twenty-six, he was sent to Greece to lead the consumer products business in that market, which at the time was experiencing a significant slowdown. After managing a picture-perfect turnaround in three years, he was sent back to France as general manager for France of L'Oréal Paris before heading up the Biotherm subsidiary where he led a complete brand repositioning. Five years later, he was sent back out to the field to manage L'Oréal's German subsidiary, and from there to Asia to create the Asia zone, where the group was ten years behind its main American competitors. And in 2001, just a few days before the September 11 terrorist attacks, he arrived in New York as CEO of L'Oréal USA.

Agon's story, while exceptional because of his meteoric rise and success, is fairly typical of many Loréalian careers, built on opportunities for people to spread their wings while ensuring that they constantly return to the mother ship for strategic alignment.

It is this combination of autonomy and control, distance and proximity that is key to resonance among divisions, brands, regions, and countries. China provides a striking example because of the firm's digital success there and the country's huge digital dominance. L'Oréal's Chinese operations have turned into a living lab for all things digital throughout the group, an incredible disruptive revolution in a highly challenging market, where L'Oréal is one of the only players to have increased its market share in recent years. At the same time that it has been allowed to operate autonomously, L'Oréal China has worked hand in hand with the CDO and Paris headquarters in its digital transformation. The Chinese subsidiary has helped the company develop cutting-edge knowledge that resonates in other markets.

Because the inclinations of Chinese consumers can be seen as precursors of future behaviors in other parts of the world, the impact of L'Oréal's knowledge of these customers on the company's digital revolution is dramatic. The Chinese market functions as a highly effective laboratory in which L'Oréal can study how to develop customer profiles and optimize customer experience. Data is central to this endeavor, especially since Chinese consumers are less concerned about data protection than consumers in other parts of the world. In Lancôme stores in China, for example, sales staff are equipped with iPads to record each customer's profile and retrieve their WeChat account in order to communicate with them more effectively. L'Oréal goes even further through a partnership with Alibaba that allows it to leverage data-driven consumer analytics from Alibaba's 600 million–plus customer base.

A key aspect of L'Oréal's China digital strategy is omnichannel experience. By not just building a highly effective e-commerce business but inventing omnichannel solutions for a market where online/offline convergence is much more mature than in other parts of the world, L'Oréal China has carved out a dominant position for itself. In this effort, former CEO of L'Oréal China Stéphane Rinderknech recognizes that he was given a great deal of improvisational autonomy and allowed to take significant risks. He describes his meeting in 2012 with the CEO of e-commerce giant Tmall, Daniel Zhang, who insisted all of L'Oréal's luxury brands be included on his e-commerce platform. While this was a huge gamble and leap of faith for L'Oréal, the two men had established enough mutual trust that Rinderknech decided to go for it. The bet paid off, and L'Oréal has gained tremendously from being a privileged partner of Tmall, accessing not just its millions of consumers but its data and other digital capabilities.

To serve the company's ambitious e-commerce strategy, L'Oréal China has had to develop high-performance logistics systems to deal not just with enormous distances but also with the country's mega shopping holidays such as Singles' Day, also known as 11/11. E-commerce has now been enriched with a whole range of services such as an app that allows users to try on lipstick colors and the more recent offering by La Roche-Posay's Effaclar brand, which diagnoses acne-prone skin. All this without cannibalizing in-store sales.

The omnichannel approach used in China also pays off in the traditional retail space. Thanks to data obtained from their online transactions, customers of L'Oréal Paris and Maybelline receive alerts and offers on their phones when they approach one of the brands' counters. In the stores, several brands offer augmented-reality makeup mirrors, and QR codes enable customers to obtain information on their smartphones.

Beyond the excellent business opportunities it offers, China teaches the company to see into the future of other markets. What L'Oréal practices in the Chinese market then resonates globally and improves its positioning as a data, e-commerce, and omnichannel leader. As L'Oréal's boss in China sums up well: "We bring Parisians here to learn."

******

Throughout a digital transformation endeavor, from kickoff to implementation, the role of a leader such as Agon is to convince, motivate, and reassure people up and down the organization, one conversation at a time. In the early days of L'Oréal's transformation process, Agon opted for an improvisational approach that provided the most relevant digital solutions for each market and allowed individual executives and managers to seize the digital opportunity and make it their own. Improvisation thrives on fast-changing environments where new solutions need to be developed in real time. It also emanates in more stable environments, where experience combines with creativity and audacity to give way to new digital practices. It requires an overall culture of aesthetic forgiveness that prizes learning and accepts failure.

Lubomira Rochet's arrival signaled the resonance phase, in which she and her small cadre of digital experts intervene on an ad hoc basis by engaging in conversations, explaining, enabling, and empowering. All the while, as team members travel back and forth from the field to headquarters and back out, they facilitate the sharing of knowledge. When visiting L'Oréal headquarters in Clichy, right outside Paris, teams from around the world are greeted with a sign on Rochet's door that captures her spirit and the source of her early inspiration: "Welcome to Silicon Clichy!" Conversations resonate throughout the organization, making the digital strategy highly dynamic and adaptive to fast-changing technology and market demands. Transformation rolls out through the entire organization in the manner of a compelling wave of change that overtakes resistance.

TRANSFORMATION TIPS

- Accept and communicate that digital transformation is all-encompassing; nothing will remain unchanged.
- Designate an evangelist-in-chief who will inspire the rest of your organization.
- Give people in your organization time to make sense of the changes ahead by encouraging small projects that embody the ambitions of individual teams and can inspire others.
- Accept ambiguity and blurriness at first. A roadmap may take time to emerge and to be formalized, and the process will require the right leader.
- Be transparent and communicate frequently, both formally and informally throughout your company so everyone can participate.
- Know that mistakes will be made; failure will happen.
- Embrace resonance—allow ideas and knowledge to travel and inspire.
- Do not underestimate how difficult change can be for individuals and their teams.

CULTIVATE HEALTHY DOUBT

A visit to "Silicon Clichy," as L'Oréal's offices outside Paris have been dubbed, offers L'Oréal executives posted around the world a welcome opportunity to reimmerse themselves in headquarters culture. Such visits can also lead to disconcerting conversations. Then-Canada CMO Stéphane Bérubé tells the story of an unsettling meeting with CEO Jean-Paul Agon: "We had had a good year of growth and the share (price) was very high. We were expecting a big thank-you and congratulations from our CEO, which he did, but he also said, 'Everything you do is wrong, and we need to change everything.'"[1] Later, having gotten over his initial shock, Bérubé realized that change was not just required, it was urgent, and yes, it had to include everything from how they went to market, to the media mix, to the way they related to consumers. The story captures one of L'Oréal's most distinctive and deeply engrained cultural beliefs: no matter how well things are going, there's always an urge to do better or differently. We call it the practice of deliberate disruption.

Throughout his tenure as CEO, Agon has deliberately increased the amount of disruptive pressure within the organization: "For me, disruption is something positive: it's the kind of total transformation that changes everything. Change opens up opportunities to challenge yourself. It takes these kinds of disruptive moments for the smartest and most agile companies to hit the accelerator."[2] As we showed in Chapter 1, Agon doesn't just embrace the kind of disruption that throws everything up in the air, he orchestrates it deliberately.

While the term *disruption* belongs to twenty-first-century management-speak, the basic notion of deliberately disrupting your thinking or your business is deeply engrained in the history and culture of L'Oréal. It is tied to a key feature of the L'Oréal mindset going back to the company's early years, the exercising of "healthy doubt."

Productive Anxiety

In his 2001 memoir, *L'Aventure L'Oréal,* François Dalle, L'Oréal's CEO during the greater part of the twentieth century, reflects on the anxiety he and his predecessor, Eugène Schueller, shared about their competitors. "We should always be mindful that others may be just as intelligent, ingenious and knowledgeable as we are. . . . Over the course of my 45 years at L'Oréal, I never stopped being afraid of our competitors and was always eager to spread the fear around me."[3] He cites Schueller as saying: "Business is tough, at night you go to sleep with concerns on your mind, it's like a thorn in your side that's there with you at all times, and when you wake up, it's still there." Beyond the competitive environment, the political and economic instability of the interwar era, the deep chaos of World War II, and the fast-changing needs of consumers surely weighed on Schueller and then Dalle.

Of course, Schueller's preoccupations went beyond running L'Oréal and were tied to the upheaval that rocked France from the 1920s to the mid-1940s, including the German occupation. The record is clear that he was closely associated with the extreme right group La Cagoule, and actively collaborated with the Nazis during the occupation. The war years do not constitute a proud moment in the history of L'Oréal and its founder. Ten years after the war, Schueller, who had been denounced as a collaborator but managed to escape conviction, passed the CEO baton to François Dalle. Dalle inherited much of Schueller's business anxiety, sometimes bordering on paranoia, as he later related in a humorous anecdote that took place in the 1950s. Having heard rumors that L'Oréal's German competitor Schwarzkopf was entering the French market, Dalle directed his team to develop a massive campaign to promote the products on which the two companies were competing.

It wasn't until weeks later that someone clarified that it was in fact the German soprano Elisabeth Schwarzkopf who was scheduled to wow Parisians. High anxiety!

The term that is now used within L'Oréal to refer to this pervasive anxiety is "healthy doubt," or *saine inquiétude* in French. Former CEO Lindsay Owen-Jones, who ran L'Oréal from 1988 to 2006, often used it, including in this interview: "I maintain an attitude of healthy doubt that mobilizes and stretches our efforts. Every morning, I tease out tensions, I caution people, I draw their attention. . . . I see it as my responsibility to call out a division that's inclined to complacency or unrealistic optimism."[4] Later he added, "I'm never satisfied and never convinced we are winning. I try to convince my people we might not be."[5] One of the aims of the healthy doubt approach is to throw people off kilter and test their ability to defend their position.

The healthy doubt attitude is deeply rooted in the company's identity, as evidenced by the common use of the expression in L'Oréal-speak. Agon recently commented on the group's response to the threat of new entrants into the digital ecosystem, echoing Dalle's own words about his sleep patterns: "This kind of threat helps us cultivate and maintain healthy doubt. It doesn't keep us up at night, but the minute we wake up, it's on our minds. The best way to deal with the threat is to stay ahead of it and to be the ones disrupting the market. The best way to win the race is to go ahead and accelerate."[6]

The association in Agon's mind between healthy doubt and disruption is suggestive: anxiety that pushes you a step ahead of the market is productive.

Challenging the Status Quo

At L'Oréal today, healthy doubt is about challenging the status quo; it is a process of permanent questioning, discussion, and even confrontation that is both systematic and recurrent, but can take many forms. One example is store visits, a longstanding custom among generations of L'Oréal executives, one that Agon has embraced with great enthusiasm. Here's a media account of one of his trips to the East Coast as he was leading a group of twenty or so mostly French executives on a field trip across New Jersey malls: "Methodically, they moved through Garden State Plaza in Paramus, pausing to hear managers give a rundown on their businesses or to huddle around a competitor's counter and trade notes, as the group caravanned from one brand to another through Macy's, Sephora, Kiehl's, the Body Shop, Nordstrom and Neiman Marcus."[7]

Store visits have several purposes for a CEO like Agon. They help him keep his finger on the pulse of the sector, and make sure that his senior executives do the same. But they are also meant to serve as reality checks or possibly to trigger and promote the doubtful and disruptive moments he favors so much. This is all part of what he refers to as organized chaos: "For many, many years, our competitors—especially in the US—called us a kind of 'organized chaos,' because for them, we are not very organized. It's intentional, because it allows us to always keep our mind open to new ideas, ready to jump on new trends and take new opportunities."[8]

Permanent Questioning

There is no question that Agon's healthy doubt served as an early warning system for the incoming digital tsunami, as it had over the years for previous CEOs encountering major contextual shifts. In the case of Agon, the acceleration of change over the course of his tenure has made the deeply engrained approach never to take success for granted particularly adaptive and effective.

In the 1960s, Dalle, having tired of unproductive meetings, decided to inject an element of tension into routine meetings. He was so convinced of the need for disruption that he renamed a large headquarters board room the "confrontation room." He would select people from across the company based on their conflicting opinions or agendas, and bring them together for staged confrontations. Typical tensions revolved around issues such as local adaptation versus global brand strategy, perfection versus speed to market, and scientific research versus market-driven product development.

While the confrontation room was decommissioned a decade ago, a culture that encourages tension still permeates the organization. Recent evidence suggests, however, that the longstanding love for tension may itself be falling prey to healthy doubt. This time, it is this deeply anchored cultural feature itself that is being challenged within the context of a sweeping effort to make the culture more inclusive and collaborative in line with digital transformation. One of the eight core messages of the recently introduced Simplicity manifesto is "Cooperation is the new confrontation." Collaboration, diversity, and inclusiveness are increasingly at the top of the agenda, following best practices, current management theory, and societal changes, according to which building bottom-up shared purpose and trust is healthier and more effective than nurturing conflict and confrontation.

This doesn't mean that tensions should not be voiced, quite the contrary. Tensions and conflict are indispensable elements of a healthy culture that promotes trust, accountability, and commitment. Unless managers can debate, challenge, and question decisions, they are unlikely to commit fully or to feel accountable. The trick is to allow tensions and conflict to surface in a way that supports rather than shuts down collaboration. None of the group's inherent contradictions embodies the cult of tension better than the one between R&D and marketing.

From the early days of L'Oréal, research and marketing have been intertwined: Eugène Schueller invented by night the products he sold to hair salons by day. Throughout his life, he combined his devotion to scientific research and his passion for communication and marketing. Some have argued that he brought marketing to France. He expressed his ambition clearly upon registering his patent, in 1928, for a hair dye with rapid application and results: "The era of charlatanism is over. Science will replace empiricism." From then on, L'Oréal espoused traditional science without abandoning market-driven inspiration and creativity. This is a company that embodies the paradox between science and art.

The Dual Innovation Channel

Just a few years after Schueller filed his first patent, in 1935, a young female chemist working in a L'Oréal research lab, Mademoiselle Galissot, whose first name history has unkindly failed to preserve, invented an oil containing benzyl salicylate, a substance capable of filtering and absorbing ultraviolet rays. In 1936, supported by a sizable promotional budget, the oil, branded Ambre Solaire, was launched, just in time for the passage of law guaranteeing a long-awaited benefit for all French workers: a full two weeks' annual paid holiday. Sun protection for your holiday? A perfect intersection of scientific innovation and market needs!

This double anchoring in research and marketing would later, and to this day, be known in the group as the "dual innovation channel." Marketing is the so-called direct or "inductive" channel, as François Dalle called it. It's about identifying needs, trends, and social and cultural change, and challenging the labs to find formulas that will get the job done. Research, on the other hand, leads the "reverse" channel and brings about innovation for the sake of innovation, which is then passed on to marketing, where it comes to life as a product.

Balancing Passion with Science

Throughout L'Oréal's history, drive and passion have lived alongside science and rigor in a balancing act, at times leading to tension and instability. In the early 1950s in-house researchers had lost their research drive: they had apparently let arrogance and routine get in the way of their efforts and closed themselves off to the rest of the company, leading to poor performance. Passion and drive had yielded to complacency and boredom. In response to this sorry state of affairs, Dalle created an advanced research department with the main objective of developing fundamental research alongside the existing applied research labs, setting up a model of competition, if not outright confrontation, that remains to this day.

The two departments complemented each other well—one focused on scientific discovery while the other responded to the needs of consumers. In one instance, a researcher from the fundamental research department invented a formula to help fine hair hold its shape. Its unfortunate side effect was that hair would lose its pigmentation. Applied researchers turned the side effect into a positive feature and created Inoa, a line of ammonia-free coloration products.

The fundamental research department attracted world-class scientists while protecting them from the pressures of product development. By definition, fundamental research requires time and patience. On the other hand, breakthroughs demand to be tested, their scope validated, and formulas finalized before they can be incorporated into products. Fundamental researchers often complained of the lengthy market testing processes their applied colleagues insisted on. Again, passion collides with rigor.

Meetings were held weekly between the two research entities, often facilitated by the CEO, in order to air out tensions and encourage joint efforts. The company learned the challenges and virtues of freely expressing opposing viewpoints, eventually and grudgingly leading to productive collaboration.

Throughout his career, Dalle remained a strong promoter of fundamental research and the legitimacy it affords the company. At an annual shareholders meeting, Dalle, certainly not a scientist himself, vehemently refuted the accusation that L'Oréal had turned into little more than an advertising company. "Advertising," he hammered, "is there to promote our breakthroughs and to tout the scientifically proven efficacy of our products. Under no circumstances should it be used to hide their shortcomings."[9]

Tensions and Achievements

Many things have changed today: the global L'Oréal marketing machine has been honed using sophisticated techniques and strategies; products and brands have multiplied exponentially; and budgets have dramatically increased. Research has become multidisciplinary and includes both fundamental and applied approaches. Specialized research centers and labs are scattered throughout the world, and the number of researchers has gone from fewer than 100 after WWII to 3,600. Multidisciplinary research teams representing sixty nationalities work across thirty or more research domains and are spread across nineteen research centers worldwide. L'Oréal applies for more than 600 patents every year. It is often difficult for the outside observer to comprehend the full logic of how these different units fit together. The truth of the matter is that there is in fact duplication of efforts and, as a result, built-in and deliberate competition.

In recent years, some research efforts have shifted focus away from products to include services, artificial intelligence–enabled immersive experiences, and personalized products and services such as Makeup Genius, the virtual makeup try-on app, or the clip-on My Skintrack UV, which measures the wearer's sun exposure. As technology-driven research takes on a greater role in the company's innovation strategy, the decades-long tension between research and marketing has extended beyond the chemistry and biology labs to the tech research units. At the core of this tension is the very question of the firm's function—it is about creating value by developing solutions that resolve consumers' problems and fulfill their needs. The push-and-pull debate between the two is a driver of dynamism and ensures a constant state of readiness to challenge and justify. Nowhere is this better illustrated than in the annual "pipeline" meeting, an internal market in which R&D professionals present and "sell" their new formulas to brand leaders. An innovative product or service is only as valuable as its ability to gain the attention of a brand that sees the fit with its own customers' needs, and is willing to take it on and invest in bringing it to market.

Market Leader and Challenger

Another noteworthy strategic tension at L'Oréal that acts as a source of change and disruption is its ability to behave both as a market leader and a challenger.

Worldwide Leader

L'Oréal reached worldwide market leadership in 1986, under CEO Charles Zviak, and has kept this position ever since. Unfortunately, Zviak, a staunch proponent of scientific research, was only able to savor this significant achievement briefly as he remained in the CEO seat less than three years because of ill health. With growth rates above sector average, the L'Oréal group has been able to strengthen its position consistently. To a journalist asking, "So, what's the point of being world leader?" then-CEO Lindsay Owen-Jones, who succeeded Zviak, replied, "There isn't one! I personally never mention our leadership status. These titles are bestowed by analysts and journalists, maybe because there are so few sectors where France is a world leader. Look at Clarins, 25 or 30 times smaller than we are. Their development is remarkable."[10]

Jean-Paul Agon commented in a personal interview on the group's ambivalent relationship with its competitors: "L'Oréal has always had a certain fascination, some might say admiration, for other companies and brands, including its competitors—this in spite of the merciless competition in the sector." We are again reminded of Schueller and Dalle's anxieties. Agon compared this combination of admiration and competitiveness to the kind of sportsmanship that exists in athletics: "To be and to remain a world champion, you have to work hard and then harder."[11]

L'Oréal is on a constant quest to outrun its competitors, accumulating brands, products, and market segments to fulfill its vision of "beauty for all." Titles such as world leader are the icing on the cake, in truth much less meaningful than the actual performance. This kind of performance requires thinking like a challenger, always fighting for that next bit of business and never taking success for granted. Performing this way is very much about healthy doubt: nothing is really ever good enough; there is always room for a greater challenge. When L'Oréal acquired Kiehl's in 2000, much of the thinking behind the acquisition was to make Kiehl's an internal challenger that would serve as a wakeup call and trigger a different way of thinking and reinventing marketing for L'Oréal's brands. Owen-Jones implored his marketing executives: "Don't break the Kiehl's model, it has a lot to teach you."[12] In other words, let's preserve the Kiehl's model and learn from it rather than forcing the company to adapt to our ways. Before Agon, Owen-Jones was a keen disruptor himself.

The acquisition of Kiehl's is but one striking instance of deliberate disruption to the company's well-oiled marketing machine. In recent years, digital transformation has made the disruption of marketing practices an ongoing requirement in response to a broad range of market-disruptive events ranging from technological acceleration to the rise of indie brands, increasing consumer power, and, more recently, the COVID-19 pandemic.

The market challenger's state of mind is prevalent among current and past executives. Here is the scene of our meeting with Frédéric Rozé, then CEO for North America, on a top floor of L'Oréal's New York City headquarters.[13] The office is filled with products and promotional material from the group's many brands. Rozé quickly sidesteps our question about L'Oréal's history in the United States and its many successes on its competitors' home turf: "As surprising as it may seem, for L'Oréal the U.S. is our largest emerging market." He embarks on a passionate explanation of what it takes to win over and retain each of the company's seventy million customers in the U.S., and to address the diversity of their needs and preferences. This determination has only grown in the digital era. As both independent beauty brands and the so-called GAFA (Google, Amazon, Facebook, and Apple) big-tech players have disrupted the market, L'Oréal has maintained its determination to ward off the competition by leveraging its competitive advantages old and new: its understanding of the market, its R&D excellence, and, more and more, its ability to extract value from data.[14]

According to Agon, digital competition has served to galvanize his troops: "It's true that at L'Oréal, we really want to be the pioneers of this new age, this new world. And so, in terms of digital, in terms of AI, in terms of fast prototyping, in terms of everything, we want to be the leading front!"[15]

Challengers at Heart

On January 17, 2017, L'Oréal China CEO Stéphane Rinderknech presided over a glamorous event at Shanghai's Exhibition Center, to celebrate the twentieth anniversary of the group's entry into the Middle Kingdom. Rinderknech and his bosses and colleagues at L'Oréal had much to celebrate that day. L'Oréal had reached an undisputed leadership position in the Chinese market thanks to fifteen flagship brands across its four divisions. With two manufacturing plants, a state-of-the art R&D center, and headquarters in Shanghai, L'Oréal China had become the second-largest diamond in L'Oréal's crown, having eclipsed France, the company's home market, just the year before.

In true L'Oréal fashion, however, twenty years after its late entry into the Chinese market, L'Oréal still saw itself as a challenger. Procter & Gamble, Shiseido, and Estée Lauder had all preceded it into China and managed to stake out their own market leadership early on. Rinderknech recalled that L'Oréal had set out to reach a clear and inspiring objective upon entering China: to put a lipstick in the hands of every Chinese woman,[16] an ambitious goal it was well on its way to achieving. At the time, China offered a great opportunity to take on such a challenge, as there were no dominant domestic brands, meaning that market leadership was up for grabs among the leading international beauty giants.

L'Oréal China adopted typical challenger practices: innovating for local consumers, mining untapped markets and segments, defying conventional wisdom, and embracing the learning opportunities that come from doing things differently.[17] Thanks to heavy investment from the get-go, L'Oréal China enjoyed fast and steady growth in its first decade. Important milestones in the history of L'Oréal China illustrate its rollercoaster ride along the way. In 2004, the company doubled its year-on-year sales, with a vertiginous climb from $180 million to $380 million. Capitalizing on this success, it made two acquisitions that year. One, Yue Sai, was a slightly faded luxury brand started by a Shanghai socialite who wanted to bring makeup to a country where it had been banned or frowned upon for many decades; the other, Mininurse, gave L'Oréal a foothold in the bottom end of the mass-market skin care segment. Each of the two brands came with its own manufacturing facility, a significant advantage for an international player looking for a long-term position in the market.

On the heels of these acquisitions, the company opened an R&D center near Shanghai in 2005 with a view to developing products that were better suited to the needs of Chinese consumers. However, in spite of these investments and many successes, the company found it hard to grow some of its core mass market brands, and had to pull hair and body care brand Garnier out of the market in 2014 due to the intense competition from other international brands and from the increasingly powerful Chinese mass market brands. The Mininurse acquisition proved tricky and jeopardized L'Oréal's near-perfect run as an integrator of brands (although Body Shop has also contributed to the less-than-perfect record). More sizable and successful was the 2014 purchase of Magic Masks, a leader in the fast-growing and competitive facial beauty mask category, and another opportunity for L'Oréal to solidify its ties to the Chinese market and to export Chinese products to its other markets. L'Oréal's spectacular success in China has been fueled almost exclusively by its luxury and mid-tier products, these segments representing the fastest growing in the market thanks to the phenomenal growth of the Chinese middle and affluent classes.

L'Oréal's second decade in China has been marked by the country's fast economic growth and the spectacular development of its digitally enhanced economy. Again, the challenger posture paid off in a very dynamic context, allowing Rinderknech and his colleagues to take calculated risks and position themselves at the forefront of the country's digital consumption revolution, placing early winning bets on emerging phenomena such as Singles' Day, the rapid dominance of the BAT trio (Baidu, Alibaba, Tencent), the accelerating potential of so-called lower-tier cities, and the transition to a cashless economy.

One of the greatest accolades for the company is public recognition by its Chinese partners, including the 2019 award it received from Alibaba for best digital transformation across sectors, a true sign of the profound integration of L'Oréal in the Chinese retail ecosystem.

Today, as it reaps the rewards of its challenger strategy by celebrating L'Oréal Paris's number-one position across categories and Lancôme's leadership in the luxury category, rather than gloating about its successes, L'Oréal maintains the learning posture of a market challenger. CDO Lubomira Rochet refers to the Chinese market as a "laboratory" for L'Oréal: "The habits, the consumption patterns out there are really phenomenal . . . there is no difference between on and offline, it's a continuum of experiences. The magnitude of the change has been tremendous . . . everything we see coming from China we think will spread out."[18] At no time has this comment been more dramatically true than during the COVID-19 pandemic. Having experienced massive lockdown ahead of other countries, China provided many important learnings and practices that were later successfully applied to other L'Oréal markets around the world.

It is this profound admiration, sometimes bordering on giddiness for the opportunities the Chinese market and its digital giants have to offer, that is most indicative of L'Oréal's challenger approach to China and to the disruption it has afforded the company. In this posture we find clear traces of the company's deeply engrained healthy doubt and embrace of conflict and confrontation. Disruption is actively sought as a way to bring out the best in the company's talents and its ability to reinvent its ways.

Whereas L'Oréal was a late entrant into China, it ventured into Japan very early, just fifteen years after the end of WWII, at a time when Japan remained an isolated and protectionist market. In the early 1950s, Dalle sent a young French couple, Jacqueline and Maurice Arnal, both chemists, to Japan to explore the market, with a brief to focus on understanding the potential for hair color. This somewhat unusual market discovery approach suggests a realization that entering Japan would require caution, respect, and patience and was first and foremost a human adventure.

The young couple soon identified a Japanese manufacturer to partner with and opened an office in Tokyo. It was the beginning of a lengthy learning process for L'Oréal: every single aspect of the market operated in a way that was different, from consumer behavior to competition and distribution, as well as the way negotiations are conducted, business partners are entertained, and more. The needs of Japanese consumers differed in many ways, as did the very meaning to them of beauty and care products. Although early commercial results were impressive for a newcomer, they were disappointing given the importance of the market at the time, the third-largest accessible one after Europe and the United States. It wasn't until the 1990s that L'Oréal was able to reap the benefits of its slow and patient investment in Japan and to experience significant commercial success.

In Japan, as in many other foreign markets, it is with hair products that the group first established its market leadership. Not until the mid-1990s, forty years after its initial entry into Japan, and after having severed its ties with its original joint venture partner, did L'Oréal take control of its distribution and launch research and development facilities focused specifically on the needs of Japanese consumers. In a way, that lengthy period was one of deliberate, patient, and careful observation and assessment. From there, things evolved quickly. The acquisition of Shu Uemura in 2004 propelled Japan to the number-three position worldwide among L'Oréal's markets. After decades of investment, Japan turned from the company's ugly duckling into a beautiful swan, even becoming a strong export market, thanks to its product development and production facilities.

While L'Oréal's "easy does it" approach in Japan contrasts markedly with its China strategy, the two case studies serve to illustrate a similar challenger mentality that has enabled it to position itself as a leader in markets with heavy competition from both domestic and major multi-national players. Keen observation, internal questioning and evaluation, and a healthily anxious mindset have paid off in these two markets. Agon's current ambition to lead the beauty tech market is very much driven by the same challenger mindset, a point he underlines as follows: "Five years ago, if we thought we had seen everything with the internet, in fact, we had seen nothing."

******

As we've seen throughout this chapter, challenging and disrupting the status quo is hardly a new sport at L'Oréal. In fact, each of the four CEOs since Schueller has engineered his own disruption over the course of his tenure.

In handing over the reins of the company to François Dalle in 1957, founder Eugène Schueller predicted that Dalle would bring about "le Grand L'Oréal."[19] By this, he meant that Dalle would be able to increase L'Oréal's reach and performance exponentially. In today's business language, we would refer to this as scaling. Scaling is not just about growth, it is about efficiency, about making each resource unit deliver more value, a change that often requires significant disruption. Unless an organization is able to challenge itself to create value in a different way, a way that reimagines the value creation mechanisms of a company, it may be growing but it is not scaling. Dalle scaled by expanding into different categories and sectors, such as luxury, by turning the company into a research and development behemoth, and by expanding into international markets in which the company's brands and know-how allowed it to outperform not just its competitors but its own traditional markets.

After Dalle and following Zviak's short tenure, British CEO Lindsay Owen-Jones, a typical L'Oréalian in everything but nationality, disrupted the very French company by turning it into a multinational. Anyone who has worked at a French company understands the disruption associated with such a transformation. For Owen-Jones, entering new markets meant respecting the diversity of local perspectives and traditions while bringing true brand-building expertise. His admonishments against destroying Kiehl's particular model, as related earlier in this chapter, is a case in point.

In a way, Agon's own disruption, the digital transformation he has engineered and led, has been built on the shoulders of giants. It benefits from a century's worth of healthy doubt, challenger attitude, ability to confront (and collaborate), and a constant desire for change. Reflecting on her first few years at L'Oréal, CDO Lubomira Rochet noted, "Change is not difficult for the L'Oréalian, because he is not afraid of it. On the contrary, the desire for change is very present."[20] This desire for change is deeply anchored in the corporate culture and can be traced back decade by decade, leader by leader to the very origins of the company.

TRANSFORMATION TIPS

- Consider disruption a positive force. It provides opportunities to revitalize and develop your organization.
- Constantly question the status quo in all parts of the organization: digital transformation demands "healthy doubt." This perpetual challenging of the way things are done helps you avoid complacency and unrealistic optimism.
- Cultivate a culture that embraces paradox and seeks solutions in the gray area between the black and white.
- Remain ever alert to industry developments and the arrival of unexpected new entrants. Adopt a challenger mindset and never take market leadership for granted.
- Develop an ambitious framework that gives meaning to the change process. Implementing digital transformation involves fostering a multiplicity of projects with a clearly articulated vision; the succession of achievements, modest at first, is primed for growth.
- Ensure that everyone in the organization understands and contributes to the digital transformation. There can be no true transformation without wholesale buy-in and participation.

LEARN AND INNOVATE WITH RIGOR

At L'Oréal, change and innovation are deeply intertwined. As we saw in the previous chapters, innovation has been in L'Oréal's DNA since the early days of Eugène Schueller's experiments in his Paris apartment as a young chemist. Innovation is a fundamental ingredient of digital transformation, creating a powerful commitment toward continuous transformation and reinvention of products, services, experiences, brands, and practices. By embracing innovation, a company empowers individuals and teams to imagine and develop projects that embody their passion and drive and create greater value.

As he finished his chemistry studies at university, Schueller found the working conditions and the limited resources at his disposal less than attractive, leading him to give up on the academic world early on. He did, however, have an interesting encounter before leaving the Sorbonne University. One day, a hairdresser came into the university's pharmacy department and asked the department chair, Professor Auger, to help him develop a hair dye to cover gray hair. Having no interest in the matter, Auger asked his research assistants who among them wanted to take on the task as an after-hours project. Schueller put his hand up, and the rest is history as he began to develop hair dyes at home in his spare time.

In the meantime, though, he left the Sorbonne, having found a better-paying job at the Central Pharmacy of France, a sort of cooperative and union of French pharmacists founded in 1852 with the objective of giving pharmacists greater control over the production and distribution of pharmaceutical products. During his three years as head of compounding at the Central Pharmacy, Schueller worked at night on his newfound passion, hair dyes. He registered his first patent on November 14, 1907, and transformed his one-bedroom apartment into a laboratory. In 1908, he left his job at the Central Pharmacy and started his own business. He continued to invent formulas at night and began selling directly to hairdressers during the day. In 1909, as he needed funds to develop his fledgling business, he met André Spery, an accountant from Epernay. Impressed with the younger man's enthusiasm, energy, and drive, Spery decided to invest in Schueller's venture, and together they founded La Société Française des Teintures Inoffensives pour Cheveux (the French Company for Harmless Hair Dyes), which eventually became L'Oréal.

Eugène Schueller was clearly a born innovator and entrepreneur. Not only did he create products, he also launched and acquired many companies. His early years are a testament to his ability to seize opportunities, a talent he would continue to exercise throughout his tenure as CEO of L'Oréal. As both a chemist and a consummate marketer, Schueller possessed the knowledge and skills required to develop formulas adapted to evolving consumer needs and trends. As women adopted short, boyish hairstyles in the 1920s, dyes had to allow more frequent touchups. Later, perms required a special dye that often caused allergies. When Imédia, a new hair dying brand for permed hair, was launched in 1931, ads warned of the risk of allergic reaction and advised customers to test the product first on a small strand of hair. The brand even provided an antidote to be applied in case of a rash. The strategy worked and sales shot up.

Ever the entrepreneur, Schueller moved into the personal care sector in 1928 when he acquired French soap manufacturer Monsavon, a company that had been started shortly after World War I. Seeing a growing trend for personal hygiene, Schueller snapped Monsavon from its founder, who had run it into the ground in a matter of just a few years in spite of the initial success of the brand. Schueller came up with the idea of adding milk to the soap formula and introduced "Monsavon with milk." It took some time and lots of creative thinking, but he was able to turn Monsavon around and make it a success in less than a decade. One of his innovative ideas was to sponsor a radio song contest, a new promotional technique he would later use with other brands.

Schueller made some unlikely acquisitions over the years, some in the beauty industry and others in a variety of products, including Bakelite objects, artificial silk, and quick-drying paint. These ventures allowed him to exercise his innovative thinking and continue to experiment with creative marketing tactics. Whether Schueller passed on his talent for innovation to François Dalle and other future leaders or selected them on the basis of this talent is hard to say. There is no question that Dalle was a creative thinker and innovator in his own right and that innovative thinking became increasingly encouraged and rewarded as the company continued to thrive. As is often the case when practices and skills become part of corporate culture, they were passed from one generation to another and institutionalized through corporate development programs and extensive job mobility within the organization.

Innovators Are Most Valuable Players

The spirit of innovation that permeates all levels at L'Oréal is fostered as soon as young recruits join the company. All are encouraged to craft their own career paths and are supported in their choices.

Innovation Starts from Within

Once new talents have been brought on board, they are given field exposure and management responsibilities early on. The decentralized structure of the company makes this possible—in many ways, it functions like a series of small companies or a flotilla of vessels of all sizes, from small fishing boats to aircraft carriers, each affording opportunities to learn and develop.

Continuous formal and informal review processes mean that young talents are evaluated for their competences and potential as they respond to the initiatives that are sent their way and participate in meetings and presentations. They are assessed on their ideas and how they defend them as much as on their results, and these indicators are then examined and debated both formally and informally before any promotion. Many L'Oréalians love the fact that there is no standard career path and that they get to craft their own track according to their personal style.

In a way, one of the first innovative ventures L'Oréal employees get to work on is their own career and personal brand. As is the case with new projects, flexibility and availability are the name of the game and a strategy is only as good as the performance it delivers. While new careers are nurtured, often patiently, results also count. A commonly discussed rule of thumb is that "after three years, you know what to expect, and past the age of thirty, if you haven't already left, you know you're going to be a lifer."

Innovation Is Everybody's Business

One of the aspects of L'Oréal that makes it such a compelling workplace for many is the healthy spirit of competition it fosters. Competition goes hand in hand with the spirit of innovation and entrepreneurship that is nurtured every step of the way. Every newly minted business school graduate comes in looking to build her own path to the top by promoting her own innovative projects. Very often, different projects with similar objectives are pushed along in different parts of the company and end up competing against each other for executive airtime and for a chance to be implemented. Inefficient? Maybe. Competitive? Definitely. Bursting with creative chaos? Absolutely! But competition is so engrained in the corporate culture and is so taken for granted that it doesn't get in the way of collaboration. Jean-Paul Agon has referred to L'Oréal's corporate culture as akin to high-level competition. Just like in sports, competition lives alongside team spirit and mutual support. A dog-eat-dog culture this is not, competition notwithstanding.

With 86,000 employees, clearly articulated ambitions to conquer one billion new consumers, and a cultural preference for autonomy, entrepreneurship, expertise, networking, and informality, L'Oréal is an environment in which innovators are seen as MVPs. The company operates along a classic matrix organization in which most staff members have both a brand or division and a market reporting line. For instance, a marketer working on the Lancôme brand in China reports both to her Lancôme hierarchy and to the China leadership team. The company is also evolving toward a flatter structure and more informal working styles. Junior employees have increasing access to senior leaders and are no longer expected to communicate exclusively through their line managers. Project teams are made up of staff members of different hierarchical levels who contribute equally to the project at hand.

While every employee is a potential MVP innovator, the process of turning an idea into a viable innovation is anything but a free-for-all. No matter how trivial or important a project is, or how much attention it garners at what level of the company, innovators looking to strike out must follow certain rules and rituals without exception. As they seek to position their own big idea carefully within the group's global vision, innovators must be willing to build a clear and compelling business case and get broad-based buy-in, using a clear and comprehensive line of argument. Projects are discussed and pulled apart, refined, improved, and redrafted over and over again, subjected to studies and consultations, until they are either adopted or dropped. By increasing the flow of innovative projects and ideas that emerge from within the company, digital transformation has also decreased the odds of any given project being adopted. Internal competition is fierce.

Not all digital innovations are about beauty and glamor. Some revolve around hard-core operational improvements designed to improve efficiency. Vincent Grégoire, a line operator in the Libramont, Belgium, plant, works on packaging for mass-market hair color. Grégoire has a holistic perspective on the business he contributes to: he knew that as customer demand for a greater choice of colors increased, his plant would have to manufacture a larger number of single colors in smaller batches. He was very clear on what this meant for him personally: his packaging line was making more frequent changes from one batch to the next, which reduced productivity significantly. He came up with an idea to increase efficiency by optimizing the packaging line changeover from one product to the next. He built a business case and pitched the idea to the plant's operations leadership. Having successfully made his case, Grégoire ended up working with management and some of the plant's external partners to develop an app that optimized every step of the process of switching from one color to the next in the packaging line. In commenting on his innovation experience, Grégoire emphasized that digital transformation is everybody's business and requires taking risks: "If it doesn't work, so what? You have to be willing to try things." The spirit of Eugène Schueller is alive and well.

What Vincent Grégoire's story points to is an environment that encourages bottom-up innovation, a highly desirable trait for any company. On the other hand, evidence suggests that companies do best when they can combine bottom-up and top-down approaches to innovation.[1] And managing this exchange is the role assumed by CDO Lubomira Rochet, who sees herself first and foremost as an accelerator of digital innovation. This balancing act between top-down and bottom-up innovation is best described by Rochet's boss, Jean-Paul Agon, commenting on the CDO role: "We needed to bring in a boss at the executive level to orchestrate and guide the flow of energies. And at the same time to let this energy express itself, to share the initiative with our employees, otherwise the energy flow would just dry up."[2]

Do, Undo, and Redo

Among the expressions commonly used at L'Oréal, "Do, undo, and redo" is particularly popular, and one that has resonated strongly in the digital era. Interestingly, this philosophy originated with and was frequently invoked by François Dalle, a man well ahead of his time in many ways—from his early and impressive marketing approach to his very modern approach to risk-taking in product development. Both the right to fail and the "test and learn" approach were deeply embedded in the identity of the company before they became promoted by management gurus and the lean start-up culture as elements of innovation. The lean start-up methodology aims at using hypothesis-driven testing along iterative test-and-learn cycles to speed up product development. With shorter development times, failing becomes less onerous and is seen as an opportunity to learn and perform better in the future.

Right to Fail

As we've seen, Eugène Schueller's story is clearly that of an entrepreneur who was not afraid of failure. His successor, François Dalle, turned this attitude into a corporate doctrine and even went as far as to talk about the right to fail in his memoir.[3] Dalle writes: "Executives who are true business professionals know from personal experience that there is no better way to gain expertise than to overcome your own mistakes. Some of my mistakes have remained legendary in our company, such as when I got us into the razor blade business at one point."[4] Dalle argues that the right to fail goes hand in hand with audacity. Without one, you can't expect the other to flourish, and audacity is clearly needed for innovation to thrive. Jean-Paul Agon also embraces the right to fail: "Every innovation is by definition a bet. Every launch is a bet. It's like a new movie or a new music. You never know in advance, but that's the magic of it!"[5]

Dalle institutionalized the right to fail so thoroughly that he even set up a reserve fund to cover losses associated with failed projects. While the technique may raise eyebrows among finance and accounting experts, it underscores how serious the company's CEOs were and continue to be about innovation and risk-taking and how culturally engrained these activities are. The reserve fund practice, although decidedly unusual at the corporate level, must also be understood in the context of a highly decentralized organization in which a number of start-up ventures are constantly being greenlighted at lower levels in the organization and risk is mitigated at the corporate level through diversification. A local manager wanting to preserve her P&L may well decide to put money aside to mitigate the risk associated with one or more of the riskier ventures she has agreed to sponsor.

Don't Cry Over Spilled Milk

Whereas Dalle asserted the right to fail, it is under the stewardship of Lindsay Owen-Jones that L'Oréal adopted a more systematic approach to learning from failure. As innovation accelerated and product launches multiplied, the ability to quickly draw takeaways from successes as well as failures rose in importance. OJ, as Owen-Jones was universally known within the company, was fond of keeping a count of the product launches he had contributed to: "I can easily recall the 5,000 product launches I have personally experienced in my nineteen years so far at the company. And, then there are the 10,000 other cases that I know we've experienced and learned from."[6]

But the postmortem of failed launches was always kept to a minimum. Commenting on the successful innovation culture under OJ, a reporter suggested that "audits and budget meetings are constant and do not focus on the spilled milk of the past, but hunt for leading indicators of how things will look at year-end."[7] This comment captures L'Oréal's approach to innovation perfectly—it is a well-oiled machine that moves faster than any of its competitors' and is fueled by expert market knowledge, rigorous research and development, and a highly disciplined and ruthless business approach to managing a portfolio of diversified bets across divisions. What gives any individual employee the right to fail is that her idea is one of many other bets being placed at any given point in time. Whether a specific idea works or not is almost irrelevant as long as the machine keeps its momentum. Timing is everything.

In 2011 L'Oréal dipped a toe into the market for cosmetic devices by acquiring Pacific Bioscience, the manufacturer of Clarisonic electronic beauty brushes for at-home facials. Market research showed a strong trend toward what is now known as beauty tech, and Clarisonic gave L'Oréal a turnkey opportunity to gain early mover advantage. Sadly for L'Oréal, things didn't quite go according to plan, in spite of Clarisonic's healthy sales history. Soon after the acquisition, results plateaued enough to force a plant closure. As is often the case with innovative tech solutions,[8] the brushes had achieved saturation among early adopters but failed to bridge the chasm and draw a broader majority of customers, who needed more time to discover and value the benefits of do-it-yourself facials. In summing up the takeaways, Agon provided a sober and rigorous assessment of the situation: "Clarisonic was a very interesting new adventure for us. If you think of cosmetic devices, probably in the next 10, 20 or 30 years, a cosmetic device will be part of the beauty industry in general. For us, to make a step in this direction was very interesting and very important. We are learning a lot, thanks to this acquisition, but the business is a bit more difficult than we thought."[9]

While L'Oréal announced in June 2020 that the Clarisonic brand and its operations would be shut down, the acquisition contributed significantly to the overall development of beauty tech for the company. While not a failure per se, the example of Clarisonic is indicative of the company's approach to innovation and its ability to learn from its errors, and to absorb temporary losses when they can be justified within a longer-term strategic approach.

Test and Learn

L'Oréal's century-old "Do-Undo-Redo" culture still influences current practices of test-and-learn associated with successful innovation and digital transformation. Test-and-learn is part of a broader tendency by successful innovators to bring a rigorous, data-driven approach not only to product development but to a whole range of projects or initiatives linked to strategy, operations, marketing, and, more broadly, digital transformation. The approach has been widely popularized by the success of the lean start-up methodology, which encourages faster and iterative testing phases to speed up innovation processes.

The basic premise behind test-and-learn is that the best way to know whether something will work is to test it with minimal risk exposure, collect data, learn from the test, and refine the solution to make it work better. The test-and-learn cycle can be repeated numerous times, and indeed, according to the principles of continuous improvement, should be repeated continually.

One area in which test-and-learn is used routinely is digital marketing, or "precision marketing," as it is called at L'Oréal. Digital marketing techniques have revolutionized marketers' ability to target highly specific microsegments of consumers known to have an affinity for certain types of products. Using these techniques, marketers aim to achieve both short-term effects, such as driving sales of new products, and longer-term effects, such as engagement with the brand.

The YSL marketing team in Hong Kong was looking to try out new social media technology introduced by YouTube to drive both sales and longer-term engagement. The technology makes it possible to "split" the consumer's mobile screen and display an ad for a specific product (aimed at driving sales) while at the same time showing engaging branded videos (aimed at driving engagement). Larry Luk, L'Oréal Hong Kong CMO, commented on how the teams who worked on the campaign used test-and-learn with this technology to target highly specific groups of millennial consumers the brand had found difficult to reach. In Luk's test, consumers were shown a YSL lipstick ad on a small part of their screen and at the same time were presented with engaging YSL-branded video content such as user-generated tutorials on the larger part of their screen.

By conducting test-and-learn iterations using the split-screen technology, Luk and his teams were able to fine-tune the targeting and messaging of their campaign, and to achieve both hard-to-reach objectives: a clear increase in sales for the advertised lipstick and a significant spike in engagement. The combined effect of the two elements also delivered the holy grail of all consumer engagement activities, an increase in the subscriber base. From a corporate perspective, local initiatives such as Luk's contribute to the myriad learning experiments that together amount to a large-scale test-and-learn strategy conducted under a wide range of conditions and with highly diversified risk.

Test-and-learn has been an essential feature of the recent development and launch process of Color&Co in the U.S. This at-home personalized hair coloring system combines the professional advice element of a salon visit with the ease of at-home application and personalization enabled by high tech. The coordination of these different elements made the development of the solution particularly complex. However, the payoff is worth the effort: the launch of the solution through direct-to-consumer channels makes it possible to collect quality data and continue to learn and optimize while building up word-of-mouth.

The specter of the Clarisonic innovation chasm looms in the Color&Co team's collective memory, but the timing of the launch just a few months before the COVID-19 lockdown has been fortuitous for the new brand. With many consumers less inclined to go out to salons, the benefits of the new beauty experience format shines through: the virtual platform allows at-home consumers to experience personalized solutions, supported by professional licensed colorists. The format is easily extendable from hair to cosmetics, and the lessons learned in the development of Color&Co will speed up the development process for sister brands in beauty.

Iterative scaling from local to global, from brand to division, and from division to division is precisely the approach to innovation and, more specifically, to digital transformation advocated by Lubomira Rochet in her role as chief digital officer: "L'Oréal is not a conceptual company, it is a very pragmatic organization where you start with a pilot and then you expand."[10] An innovative project is initiated and tested within a given market, brand, or business before it is formalized and scaled up. Rather than being centralized at headquarters or among "digital" experts, extraordinary digital expertise, informed by local intelligence and practices, is scattered throughout the organization and simply needs to be given a green light and a voice so it can benefit other parts of the company. This is another illustration of the balancing act between bottom up and top down—the ideas and initiatives percolate from the bottom up while the mechanisms that facilitate and accelerate the development and the efficient diffusion of these initiatives across the entire organization come from the top.

La Roche-Posay's My Skin Track UV is a skin patch that measures how much ultraviolet exposure a user is experiencing and sends the information to an app with an intelligent algorithm that alerts the user when their exposure is too high. Based on its knowledge of the user's skin and level of exposure, the app also makes personalized product recommendations for sun protection products. After initial test-and-learn iterations through partner dermatologists in the U.S., the product was released direct to consumers, first in the U.S. and eventually throughout the world. For the La Roche-Posay brand, it is an important first step into the market for services and a chance to address an important public health issue.

We've seen how the combination of a decentralized structure enabling lots of small-scale experiments and a culture that allows failure and favors a test-and-learn approach results in an environment in which people are encouraged to try new things, risk is mitigated, and knowledge and practices can diffuse efficiently to respond to fast-changing environments. So critical to the company's culture is the test-and-learn approach that it is one of the eight practices that constitute the Simplicity manifesto, the 2017 charter for the development of a more collaborative, consumer-centric, and agile culture.

The recent COVID-19 crisis has put this new culture and the practices that come with it to the test by challenging many L'Oréal markets around the world to quickly adapt to an overnight shift away from retail and toward e-commerce. Lubomira Rochet commented on the overall success of the effort: "In e-commerce, we achieved in eight weeks what it would have otherwise taken us three years to do."[11] Driven by its strong success in e-commerce in China, L'Oréal was able to adapt to the quasi-global lockdown by quickly scaling its e-commerce capabilities in markets in which e-commerce had not yet gained traction, including Latin America (300 percent growth in April 2020) and Africa and the Middle East (400 percent growth).

Incubators as Promoters of Change

If the typical L'Oréalian executive was a Frenchman who entered L'Oréal straight after business school and ran several local markets before returning to Paris to run a division, Guive Balooch, the global vice president in charge of L'Oréal's Tech Incubator, is living proof that things have changed. Balooch is a Bay Area man who, after earning a PhD in biomaterials at UC San Francisco and completing a postdoc at Stanford, was well on his way to a prestigious academic career. His parents had emigrated from Iran to the United States, and Balooch had inherited his passion for science and research from his father, a professor at Berkeley. He "fell into beauty," as he likes to put it, after growing somewhat disillusioned with the pace of innovation in his lab and deciding to explore new horizons that would allow him to "truly make a difference in people's lives."

Balooch joined L'Oréal in Chicago as a researcher working on the development of ethnic hair products and quickly took a liking to the "other side" of the business—the branding, the marketing, the consumer angle. Moving further east, to New York, he began working with academic scientists on the co-development of innovative products and solutions. Finally, in 2013, having come to the realization that innovation was more likely to come from outside the academic world and required access to a broader ecosystem, he founded L'Oréal's own tech incubator, which he now heads up from his double base in Clark, New Jersey, and, having ventured even further eastward, Paris.

Balooch is not the typical L'Oréalian, for sure; but then again, appearances can be deceiving. His background is in many ways reminiscent of the driven, entrepreneurial, scientist/marketer characters that have shaped L'Oréal's history. He also incarnates a more contemporary image of the typical L'Oréalian: multicultural, passionate, and driven by a strong commitment to make a difference by making beauty more accessible to more diverse people around the world. Recently, the original Tech Incubator has spawned new centers in San Francisco and Tokyo. Besides L'Oréal's own incubators, the company has built up its open innovation strategy by launching its own accelerators at Paris-based Station F and London-based Founders Factory, and by participating in investment funds through Silicon Valley–based Partech International Ventures.

Beyond their obvious roles of accessing and supporting innovative products and solutions, and publicly affirming L'Oréal's commitment as a significant player in the tech innovation ecosystem, the incubators and accelerators play an important internal role by modeling a tech-focused start-up culture. This brings us back to the bottom-up/top-down complementarity. Unless the company is able, from its very top, to convincingly portray itself as a key player in the tech start-up space, it cannot possibly inspire its tens of thousands of employees around the world to believe in the dream and to make it come true. The impact of L'Oréal's participation in CES, the Las Vegas annual mecca for all things tech, goes far beyond the public relations and networking objectives of such grand events. It also conveys an important internal message, an inspirational one, that this company is committed to its future as a tech-driven innovation leader, and that this starts with you, L'Oréal employee, wherever you are, whatever your role is.

No corporate communications campaign could have been as effective at convincing L'Oréal employees worldwide that the future of the company is digital and tech driven than the combined impact of recent successes coming out of the incubators. The first of these successes was the development and launch of MakeUp Genius as a result of an early partnership with Image Metrics, a facial recognition specialist, and later the acquisition of Canadian ModiFace. L'Oréal scored another success with the launch in 2018 of Lancôme's Teint Particulier, an in-store device that customizes foundation to match a consumer's complexion. This innovation resulted from the acquisition of Sayuki Custom Cosmetics, a small Southern California–based manufacturer of customized makeup solutions.

As was the case with the acquisitions of Kiehl's and then NYX, which challenged many L'Oréal managers' conception of marketing and helped usher in a more consumer-centric and data-driven era, these recent acquisitions and partnerships have begun to profoundly change the culture at L'Oréal. The need to collaborate with multicultural partners on fast innovation projects that involve teams from different divisions, functions, and areas of expertise has put pressure on some century-old traditions, but also found a resonance in these same traditions. L'Oréal's Simplicity manifesto, unveiled in 2016 and discussed at length in Chapter 8, acknowledges this pressure and provides a clear way forward. At the core of the manifesto lie principles of consumer centricity, collaborative work, trust and accountability, empowerment, and learning.

******

From Eugène Schueller to François Dalle, from Lindsay Owen-Jones to Jean-Paul Agon, innovation has always been at the heart of L'Oréal's successes. It is striking to see how the core distinctive elements of L'Oréal's culture of innovation have contributed to its more recent innovation successes as it transforms itself into a digital and tech giant. The ability to recognize these distinctive elements and to draw from them to transform the century-old company into a high-performing tech powerhouse has itself rested on its senior leadership's vision and their own thirst for innovation and transformation.

TRANSFORMATION TIPS

- Identify and support project initiators. They are your most valuable players, the true drivers of your digital transformation.
- Support innovation by creating venues and moments for team members to develop and pitch ideas through multiple interactions.
- Create a collaborative innovation framework for people to develop joint initiatives and solutions.
- Preach and practice "do, undo, and redo." Support risk-taking and institute a culture of failure as a key source of learning.
- Embrace a test-and-learn approach.
- Set up in-house incubators to foster a start-up spirit, and to reinforce people's ability to work agilely and collaboratively.
- Put human creativity at the core of your innovation strategy.

LISTEN WITH CURIOSITY

Among the consumer product categories that challenged brands looking to develop a greater share of e-commerce business, makeup stood out as probably the hardest nut to crack. Consumer concerns around touch-and-feel and sizing were addressed in the past decade by fashion brands that shifted consumer focus away from "I need to try it on right now" to "I can take my time and try it on in the comfort of my own home." The practice of offering free shipping and returns, easy refund credits, and good customer service helped online retailers like Zappos and fashion brands like Asos, Everlane, and luxury retailer Net-à-Porter make in-store try-ons irrelevant. Traditional brick-and-mortar fashion brands soon followed suit and offered seamless e-commerce experiences as well.

One product category still defied this new e-commerce logic: makeup. Applying makeup is harder than trying on shoes. Getting professional advice matters, and what do you do with that new mascara you just tried on once that gave you raccoon eyes? What about the social experience of trying on makeup with your best friend? The answer had to come eventually from virtual and augmented reality technology, but it took some time to get right. In early 2018, L'Oréal took a bold step into beauty technology by acquiring ModiFace, a Canadian start-up specializing in augmented reality for beauty. Using an app developed by ModiFace, consumers get to "try on" makeup or have their skin diagnosed virtually, on their mobile phones. L'Oréal executives had first come across ModiFace in developing Makeup Genius, the company's first foray into providing consumers with a virtual makeup experience. At first the technology was quirky and entertaining rather than useful and reliable, but it has now evolved into a game changer for the beauty sector, allowing users to try makeup on virtually with as much or as little privacy as they desire, and with a high degree of accuracy.

The first project soon led to a second one when ModiFace and L'Oréal R&D teams worked closely on developing Style My Hair, an app that lets users try different hair colors and styles. Behind the acquisition is a broader two-pronged growth strategy for L'Oréal: by bundling products with an extra layer of service, the company could offer up fun and productive experiences that make their products stand out, create more customer touchpoints, and allow customers greater control over their brand experience. Not only can a customer try out new styles before buying, she can also share them with her friends, use them in her profile pictures, have her own private makeover at home, or invent any number of other fun moments. In the words of Lubomira Rochet, "We are reinventing the experience of beauty, using technologies such as voice, AR and AI."[1] What Rochet doesn't identify explicitly is the second prong, the real magic bullet behind this strategy: every opportunity to engage one-on-one with users is another chance to grab data and get to know that customer and those like her better.

Beyond Style My Hair and Makeup Genius, L'Oréal has developed several new apps and retail concepts using ModiFace technology. One tech-enabled retail solution is Armani Box, a pop-up concept sited in airports and other high-traffic shopping areas. The Box is a vending machine that allows consumers to try products on virtually and receive their product without the help of a salesperson. For a luxury skin care, fragrance, and makeup brand such as Armani, licensed from designer Giorgio Armani since 1988, the Box concept is an entertaining and high-touch way to engage with international consumers. The travel retail industry, mostly airport duty-free shopping, is a highly lucrative business that thrives on enabling impulse shopping and entertaining experiences, and the Armani Box delivers on both counts, all the while collecting valuable data. The ModiFace technology enhances both in-store and at-home experience and has become an integral part of how customers across an increasing number of brands, including L'Oréal Paris and Lancôme, play with, choose, and buy makeup.

The interesting question for us is how a beauty company goes about acquiring a tech company and what they do with it once they own it. While the tech world was certainly a more distant fishing ground than any previous acquisition, venturing beyond its sector to acquire new competences and provide growth opportunities is not entirely new to L'Oréal. More than fifty years ago L'Oréal entered the field of skin care and luxury by acquiring Lancôme, an extension of L'Oréal's core business of hair and personal care products.

François Dalle believed that cosmetics would experience future significant growth without enduring as much competitive pressure (this turned out to be wrong!). In going after Lancôme, Dalle was clear that L'Oréal simply did not have what it took to compete in cosmetics unless it acquired a big brand in that sector. The move would require several major shifts in competences and culture at L'Oréal: first, from a research perspective, a shift from organic chemistry to biology, and then, from a marketing perspective, from mass distribution to luxury.

Luxury marketing for a brand such as Lancôme was at the time a far cry from what it is now; Armand Petitjean, the founder of Lancôme, articulated it best: "In this refined universe, advertising is an insult to the product, the product must talk alone."[2] The acquisition of Lancôme was, for L'Oréal, the credential it needed to gain entry into that "refined universe." Lancôme's position today as the world's leading women's luxury beauty brand, not to mention the subsequent success of L'Oréal's three other leading luxury brands—YSL, Armani, and Kiehl's—is a testimony to how successfully it has lived up to these credentials.

This same model of using highly targeted acquisition to develop the necessary knowledge and credentials to enter a new high-growth sector has been repeated over and over again. Recently, L'Oréal's knowledge acquisition strategy has morphed into a two-pronged approach. At the same time that it has refocused its appetite for acquisitions primarily on start-ups, as illustrated by the ModiFace takeover, it has also boosted its highly effective strategy of developing innovative alliances with its value chain partners. By positioning itself in recent years at the core of a global entrepreneurial ecosystem that includes French incubator Station F and British accelerator Founders Factory, the L'Oréal group has given itself ready access to new ideas and technologies as well to the nimbleness of the start-up culture. In the United States, L'Oréal's Women in Digital accelerator identifies women-led digitally native start-ups, supports them through a community platform, mentors their founders, and funds the most promising ventures. At the same time, the many strategic partnerships L'Oréal is forging both upstream and downstream, online and offline also speak volumes about its voracity for external knowledge and expertise in the digital era. The group's cultural legacy of openness and curiosity has enabled and given way to a constant craving for greater knowledge and expertise, which it seeks to satisfy within the complex ecosystems it now nurtures.

Politeness of the Heart

The history of L'Oréal is rich with colorful examples of the group's culture of listening and learning from others. From its early years between the two world wars, one of the secrets to L'Oréal's success as it grew from its roots as a small French venture was the strong human ties between its sales force and their clients, hairdressers for hair care and distributors and retailers for personal care. As is often the case, the impetus and the example come from the top. In his memoir, *L'Aventure L'Oréal,* originally published in French in 2001, François Dalle recounts his early days at the helm of Monsavon, the ubiquitous French soap brand. He identifies the one feature that made his sales force successful and labels it "politeness of the heart," which he describes as an "attentive, considerate and infinitely patient" approach.

The term "politeness of the heart," coined by French philosopher Henri Bergson in the late nineteenth century, is now closely associated with the more contemporary notion of empathy, the ability to experience another's feelings. It is a surprising and unusually human approach in the French postwar business context, which was generally more rigid and formal, and it clearly differentiated L'Oréal's business approach and culture. Dalle spent time in the field himself, supporting the sales force but also practicing his politeness of the heart and learning a great deal along the way.

A similar approach in the hair care division, early in L'Oréal's history, led to the weaving of close ties between L'Oréal and the French community of hairdressers (as they were then called), a relationship that remains exceptionally strong to this day. Thanks to this connection, L'Oréal became aware of a fascinating practice: hairdressers who worked on the transatlantic ships between France and New York carried with them large quantities of "Super Oréal Blanc," a hair bleach powder. In fact, they took with them far more of it than they were ever able to use on their customers. As it turns out, they had developed an informal import business, selling the bleach powder to their American colleagues. Translated into today's practices, this would qualify as influencer seeding, casually creating demand among an influential group of clients who then help spread the word to their broader community.

In 1954, L'Oréal launched Cosmair ("Cosmetics for Hair"), its U.S. hair care subsidiary, and began selling its hair dyes to hair professionals under the Excellence brand. This was the beginning of a long and arduous learning process for L'Oréal. Hairdressing was a very different type of profession in the United States than it was in France. No U.S. professional had achieved anything like the kind of notoriety or prestige of some of the era's big French names, such as Alexandre de Paris and his peers, whose salons were located in the so-called Golden Triangle off the Champs Elysées. Nor did hairdressers play the role of prescribers or influencers for their customers as they did in Europe. Hair products were distributed through a wide range of local and regional wholesalers, and Clairol, the leading U.S. brand, had developed a strong presence among both professionals and consumers by using the same brand name in both markets.

Not until a decade later did Dalle make an unexpected find while visiting hair salons in the U.S. As the group's hair care business had yet to take off in the U.S. and Dalle was getting increasingly impatient with his U.S. team, he took matters into his own hands and set out to practice his own "politeness of the heart" by visiting hair salons and talking to professionals and consumers throughout the U.S. One day, having visited three local salons in a suburb of New York City, he and an associate got caught in the rain and took refuge in a drugstore. Being the salesman he was, he walked around the store to get a sense of the retail setting. As he reached the hair care aisle, he was amazed to find a display of single-use containers of Excellence, the L'Oréal professional hair color product that was meant for salons only. Here was this highly sophisticated product being sold in a drugstore, directly to the average Jane, for home use! Not only that, it wasn't even properly packaged or labeled. Because it was meant to be sold only to hair salons, whose staff had been trained in how to use it, the product came with no instructions, in unbranded containers, and with no indication other than the name of the shade.

Upon investigation, Dalle learned that the owner of the drugstore had obtained the product from a neighboring salon. Of greater concern and upon further research, he found that this was far from the only case of such unintended distribution. Learning from the experience, he launched a repositioning of the product for the retail market, rebranding it Preference by L'Oréal and raising the price above its competitors based on research indicating higher performance. It was at that time that a young creative at J. Walter Thompson, the ad agency Dalle had hired to launch Preference, came up with the slogan: "Actually, I don't mind spending more for L'Oréal because I'm worth it!" None of this would have been possible had Dalle remained in his executive suite reading the same thirdhand market research as his competitors. Instead, his curiosity and passion for experiencing the market firsthand drove the Frenchman to a New York suburb to try to understand the U.S. hair care market.

Another L'Oréal CEO, Lindsey Owen-Jones, famously loved to prowl the aisles of department stores asking questions of customers and salespeople alike in search of nuggets of valuable information, including, in one case, engaging with two customers in a Chinese department store to find out how they had their hair colored before plying them with free samples. Owen-Jones would later quiz his subordinates to check on their own intimate understanding of the market, a sure way to keep everyone on their toes.[3]

These stories, now part of the L'Oréal legend, are transmitted from one generation of managers to the next, helping to reinforce the cultural belief that a firsthand, "politeness of the heart" approach to the market beats canned research reports and provides the best opportunities for serendipitous learning and innovation.

In Search of Universalization

Fast-forward fifty years to 2009, the year Jean-Paul Agon declared universalization a new strategic focus for the L'Oréal Group at its Annual General Meeting. Universalization, in Agon's view, is a new approach to globalization that builds on L'Oréal's legacy and ability to develop rich consumer insights from within, to serve all markets in their "infinite diversity." While a brand's positioning is defined and anchored at the global level, a clear understanding of local market preferences means the brand can be adapted in each market to better meet local needs and preferences. Universalization is "globalization that captures, understands and respects differences in desires, needs, beauty traditions and lifestyles in every part of the world."[4] The strategy reflects the group's deep recognition of beauty as both a universal aspiration and a reflection of human diversity across markets, cultures, ages, and more.

Of course, it would be naïve to ignore the universalization strategy's main objective of delivering a billion new customers by conquering emerging markets and gaining market share in mature economies. The goal here was to implement universalization across markets, swiftly and efficiently. Empathy doesn't mean lack of ambition! But an ambition this bold could only rest on a solidly established core competence of customer knowledge.

One of the key target markets in delivering the one-billion-consumer objective was India. In 2014, L'Oréal successfully launched Black Naturals by Garnier, a hair dye designed to hide white hair. The formula is specifically adapted to the cosmetic needs of Indian consumers, and the pocket-sized packaging makes it convenient to transport and distribute, responding to the need for frequent replenishment as distributors and retailers carry very little inventory. Much of L'Oréal's understanding of consumer hair care needs comes from the group's tightknit relationships with the Indian professional hairstyling sector, which it has helped kickstart and grow over two decades by offering stylist training programs and supporting salon promotional activities. This strategy is far from new to the group. In fact, it is a near-perfect replication of the one used by Dalle and, before him, Eugène Schueller, in the postwar years in France.

L'Oréal invested heavily in formalizing and supporting the hair stylist profession, contributing to the national curriculum and certification in hair coloring and to this day continuing to set the standards for professional hair care in France. None of this could have happened without Schueller's and then Dalle's politeness of the heart. This seemingly quaint but powerful strategy is one that has double resonance in the hair industry. Stylists are notoriously good at engaging in attentive and considerate conversations with their customers and they rival psychotherapists as great listeners. And how do L'Oréal sales forces get stylists to open up about their customers' own best-kept secrets if not by practicing politeness of the heart? This tried-and-true strategy and the empathetic competences it builds on were exported successfully from France to distant markets, including India, and to this day constitute one of L'Oréal's strongest international competitive advantages.

Interestingly, Jean-Paul Agon launched the universalization strategy exactly a year before his digital tsunami declaration. Today, the two go hand in hand. Without the ability to bring digital into the heart of each local market, digital transformation remains a theoretical exercise that stops short of its potential. On the other hand, understanding customers and local markets is immensely easier and more effective thanks to digital technologies and, in particular, the data they deliver. No market brings this reality to life better than China.

China: The Torture Test

The rapid adoption of digital and mobile technologies by a majority of the Chinese population, combined with the tremendous appetite for consumer goods after decades of deprivation, particularly in sectors such as beauty and luxury products, has made China a hotbed of constantly evolving consumer trends, delivering unprecedented performance results for brands. Chinese consumers across generations have embraced not just new product categories but also new consumption practices, ranging from the use of social media to e-commerce and digital currency. These new behaviors are enhanced exponentially when combined with traditional Chinese rituals like gift-giving on holidays such as Singles' Day (11/11), Chinese New Year, and Autumn Moon Festival. At the same time, self-indulgence and focus on personal appearance, which had been frowned upon for decades, have become common practice. Expressing their personality has become acceptable and desirable for consumers ranging from Gen-Zers trying out new hair colors or makeup styles to millennials eager to tout their disposable income and older customers combating skin aging.

These trends and the astonishing acceleration of the Chinese economy, in particular its digital economy in the past several years, have made China not just a leading market for L'Oréal but also a living lab in which all things digital can be tried out in real life. The constant test-and-learn logic of the Chinese market also makes it a high-stakes "torture test" for foreign groups.[5] Withstand the pain or get out! Out of the top-ten beauty players in the Chinese market in 2018, L'Oréal is the only one to have increased its market share.[6] Many factors are behind this success, including the group's market knowledge competencies, often cited as a key element. As a relative latecomer to the Chinese market, L'Oréal invested heavily in getting to know Chinese consumers. From its local acquisitions, to its sophisticated HR recruitment strategy of targeting young Chinese professionals who resemble their customers, to its Chinese celebrity brand ambassadors, to its strong alliances with Chinese distributors and retailers, and finally to its customer engagement strategy using influencers and social media, L'Oréal has put in place a high-performance consumer intelligence machine that delivers.

While the performance in China is itself stellar, the entire group benefits from the Chinese living lab. L'Oréal's boss in China remarks with some glee that Parisian executives come to China to learn how to "do digital." Politeness of the heart also means accepting that sometimes others know better.

Seizing What's Emerging

Competitive advantage in the form of traditional customer intelligence strategy and techniques is under increasing pressure as big data trumps one-to-one relationships and store visits. Suddenly, politeness matters less than data analytics in delivering performance. How well L'Oréal can adapt its curious listening to a data-first world is a test of how much the group really cares about understanding its customers. In fact, opportunities for L'Oréal don't reside as much in seizing emerging trends as they do in seizing new technologies, systems, and processes and integrating them into their legacy practices. This is where L'Oréal's competitive advantage of curious listening and learning can best pay off. In other words, what matters in defending competitive advantage is not the technologies and the data themselves, but the ability to integrate them into legacy practices and culture.

François Dalle was fond of reminding L'Oréal staff to "seize what is emerging." He had inherited this approach from founder Eugène Schueller, who built the business by doing just that, having gone from bringing the hair colors and styles of the early twentieth century to the average consumer, to launching the Ambre Solaire sunscreen in 1936 just as French workers were heading to the beach on their first-ever paid vacation. L'Oréal was able to capitalize on this movement, as suntan transformed from a mark of outdoor labor into a symbol of middle-class emancipation and the allure of fair skin faded.

More than fifty years later, then-CEO Lindsay Owen-Jones identified ethnic diversity as an emerging opportunity. He launched operations in Africa and began targeting the needs of ethnic minorities in Brazil, North America, and Europe with new ranges of products. In 1998, he acquired SoftSheen, a Chicago-based company specializing in products for Afro-curly hair. Almost two years later, L'Oréal bought Carson, a century-old world leader in the sector of ethnic cosmetics with a strong presence in South Africa.

These acquisitions eventually led to the creation in 2002 of L'Oréal's Institute for Ethnic Hair and Skin Research in Chicago, giving the group a strong early foothold in what has become a highly competitive worldwide market for ethnic hair and skin products. More recently, the group added to its portfolio of ethnic brands with Nice & Lovely, a mass-market Kenyan skin and hair brand, and Carol's Daughter, a New York City–based brand of natural products targeted at Black women.

While the company has recently come under attack for paying lip service to the Black Lives Matters movement,[7] it has responded swiftly and decisively by recognizing a lack of conversation with a fired Black transgender influencer and committing to creating an advisory committee and engaging in greater dialog with communities of color. As an employer, L'Oréal has drastically increased its focus on diversity and inclusion in recent years, ranking eighth in a recent independent international index.[8] While much of the company's focus is on gender and LGBTQ issues, there is growing awareness and urgency, as for many global brands, of the need to increase cultural and ethnic diversity in its workforce.

L'Oréalization

Lubomira Rochet is a relative newcomer not just to L'Oréal but also to the beauty world, and yet when you listen to her, she quotes François Dalle and Eugène Schueller as if she had worked alongside these legends. In the same way that curious listening enables the integration of new practices, it also supports the socialization—the "L'Oréalization"—of newcomers, individuals such as Rochet and organizations such as ModiFace, from whom it knows it has much to learn.

As it grew beyond its French borders and initial narrow sector, L'Oréal sought to recruit a wide range of individuals whose values, behaviors, and expectations matched those of its customers around the world in their diversity and breadth. Today, as the group wins awards for its leadership in diversity and inclusion, it is also not afraid to own up to the difficulties associated with espousing these values. Lubomira

Rochet has at times pointed out that being a young, foreign-born female member of the Executive Committee in her role as Chief Digital Officer has not always been smooth sailing, in spite of the expertise and competencies she brought into the group.

Similarly, the company has not shied away from publicly recognizing the gender pay gap and women's underrepresentation in corporate C-suites, and addressing head-on the myth that focusing on beauty does a disservice to women's rights and their ability to climb the corporate ladder. A recent highly visible German advertising campaign uses makeup products to graphically illustrate the power of women leaders, calling for efforts to increase women's access to leadership roles.[9] In one ad entitled, "This is an ad for men," a graph drawn in red lipstick asserts that profitability increases by 15 percent when women control 30 percent of management positions. While it recognizes hurdles and shortcomings, L'Oréal can also celebrate its tradition of curious listening and its ability to be responsive to change and criticism.

As part of its outside-in strategy, L'Oréal onboards thousands of new recruits every year in a process referred to internally as L'Oréalization, which mimics the kind of spontaneous socialization that takes place in schools and other communities that welcome newcomers on a regular basis. Recently, the process has been made easier and more efficient with the introduction of the Fit Culture app, or simply Fit, in response to staff members who suggested ways their own onboarding could have been made easier.

Fit, the first app of its kind to facilitate what HR professionals refer to as "cultureboarding," is available in eleven languages and allows new recruits to decode, understand, and master the company's culture, easing them into some of the group's practices. On the app, rookies follow a simple and fun path through information vignettes, games, and quizzes on entrepreneurship, agility, networking, and collaboration. Over five to ten minutes a day, they are let in on "internal secrets" (highlights, anecdotes, myths, and legends) and eventually graduate a month later as #CultureGurus.

Full Color Palette

The outside-in strategy is neither new nor restricted to individuals. It is behind many of the successful acquisitions that have fashioned the group into the diverse beauty powerhouse it is today, each brand brought in to contribute its own set of products, positioning, market knowledge, practices, distribution channels, features and benefits, and more, to feed future organic growth. Beyond the ones already cited, YSL, Shu Uemura, Kiehl's, Armani, NYX, Redken, Matrix, and many more have been added over the years. In an interesting contrast to L'Oréalization, insiders coined the term "Nyxification" to refer to the effect of the NYX acquisition on the rest of the company. A knowledge-sharing strategy was put in place at the time of acquisition. Soon after the brand was brought on board, field trips to California were organized for Paris managers to experience its digital-first magic firsthand. From product development to go-to-market strategy, social media engagement, influencer marketing, recruitment practices, and internal culture, every aspect of NYX's special approach was reverse engineered—identified, scrutinized, documented, and carried back to headquarters for diffusion across brands.

The Making of an Icon

Since its early days, L'Oréal has pursued a strategy of targeted acquisitions prompted by objectives such as gaining or reinforcing a foothold in a given market, leveraging a new distribution channel, or filling a gap in its product range. More crucially perhaps, throughout its history, L'Oréal's acquisitions have been first and foremost a source of learning. One of the most significant examples is the acquisition of Maybelline in 1996, followed by that brand's turnaround and extensive revamp into the embodiment of "Urban American Chic," as claimed in its late 1990s tagline,[10] and best exemplified by its headquarters move from Memphis, Tennessee, to New York City. The brand now stands as a world leader in makeup and sells quintessentially "made in New York" products not just in the U.S., but also in China and a hundred other countries.

Maybelline New York, as it is now known, is one of eight L'Oréal global brands that exceed $1.5 billion in sales, a real success story for this outside-in acquisition of an iconic American brand. Besides letting L'Oréal in on the secrets of American makeup consumers and providing a model for successful universalization (from a midwestern U.S. brand to a global phenomenon), Maybelline quickly delivered the goods by providing valuable expertise early on, including the know-how that allowed it to manufacture mascara at less than half the cost of its European counterparts.[11]

A Bridge Too Far

Not all of L'Oréal's acquisitions have been as successful as the Maybelline deal. In 2006, L'Oréal acquired The Body Shop, a British company founded by human rights activist Anita Roddick to pioneer the manufacturing and selling of cosmetics that take ethical, social, and environmental impact into account. The Body Shop gave L'Oréal its first retail foothold to compete with cosmetics retailers such as LVMH's Sephora and an opportunity to learn the retail business.

Eleven years later, in 2017, L'Oréal uncharacteristically threw in the towel and sold The Body Shop to Brazilian beauty giant Natura, leading many observers to wonder what had gone so terribly wrong. As is often the case, a combination of factors is to blame, including intense competition from other natural beauty brands such as L'Occitane en Provence, the advent of e-commerce, the brand's inability to refresh its somewhat dated flower-power image, and, most seriously, a huge cultural clash between the two companies. So foreign were The Body Shop's operations to L'Oréal that, throughout its ownership period, the group's annual reports detailed the retailer's activities in its own separate section, almost as an afterthought. Some have commented, not without merit, that the retail business was simply a bridge too far for L'Oréal, a questionable argument given the success of Kiehl's, a highly successful retail brand.

On closer analysis, L'Oréal's unfortunate Body Shop experience was also a learning opportunity: it offered a first glimpse into the natural products market, which it has now embraced with its Sanoflore brand. Similarly, the failed retail experience may have contributed to a much more positive outcome for the Kiehl's brand, which the group acquired in 2000 with a single store in New York City's East Village but which now ranks among the group's leading brands, with its two thousand points of sale across sixty countries. Kiehl's, in return, has contributed a creative marketing approach that has inspired L'Oréal: simple products and touchpoints delivered through owned points of sale. Beyond these takeaways, L'Oréal got to learn from the Body Shop failure itself, particularly when it comes to the integration of highly divergent cultures.

More recently, the acquisition of brands such as NYX, a Californian "digital native" makeup brand, and ModiFace has pushed the boundaries of L'Oréal's expertise and culture. NYX, a pioneer in social networks, also brought with it an innovative omnichannel approach, while ModiFace opened up the tech world for L'Oréal.

What's new for L'Oréal is the acquisition of companies outside the cosmetics industry, especially tech companies. The ModiFace takeover is a perfect case in point. The 2018 acquisition of the Canadian augmented reality (AR) start-up was an ambitious move by the group to procure a deeper knowledge of customers and develop new digital sales channels, as well as greater personalization and consumer engagement. The onus is now on L'Oréal to extract maximum value out of this acquisition by turning the technology into an enabler of a new kind of beauty experience.

Interestingly, the relationship between L'Oréal and ModiFace started as a strategic partnership in 2012, but evolved into an acquisition as the group realized that AR and AI (artificial intelligence) were about to transform customer experience and eventually the entire industry. Commented Rochet: "We decided that a partnership was not enough. We really wanted to source that capability internally. We thought AR would be a completely new way of discovering our products."[12] The increasing reliance on partnerships signals a noteworthy development in L'Oréal's strategy to bring outside knowledge into the group.

Ban the Boring

The importance of influencer marketing in promoting beauty brands and products cannot be overstated. When it comes to influencing consumers on social media, legacy brands such as L'Oréal are at a real disadvantage compared with indie brands owned by some of the world's most popular celebrities, including Kylie Jenner, Kim Kardashian West, and Rihanna. Legacy brands also struggle to find and attract the right influencers, and then to manage influencer campaigns effectively. Enter Fredrik, the other Fredrik, Didrik, and Josh, four young Swedes whose fascination with the power of influencer marketing and understanding of the disconnect between influencers and brand drove them to create Tailify, a platform that allows brands to choose their influencers, develop relevant content, and measure effectiveness.

The Tailify founders pitched to L'Oréal's open innovation team and soon launched the #bantheboring campaign for Matte Shaker Lipstick by Lancôme with four influencers. More campaigns followed, and the four Swedes now count themselves among L'Oréal's trusted partners, injecting innovative ideas, technology, energy, and know-how into legacy brands such as Lancôme.

Until recently, L'Oréal's only significant partnership had been a 2002 joint venture with Nestlé to market so-called beauty pills that promote skin and hair health. After thirteen years of lackluster sales, the project was finally abandoned in 2015. Today's partnerships with start-ups and more established players up and down the value chain follow a different logic, based on much faster and more nimble experimentation. While this logic mirrors the accelerated pace of innovation in the sector and beyond, it is anchored in the group's century-old approach of listening with curiosity and opens up a range of new learning opportunities for the group.

An Open Innovation Ecosystem

Nowhere is the "listening with curiosity" approach better illustrated than in the mission of the global open innovation team to advance ideas, methods, products, and services through knowledge sharing and creativity.[13] The team's brief is to be at the core of a beauty innovation ecosystem by setting up partnerships with individuals and teams around the world. As part of this strategy, the group took an early stake in two incubator-accelerators, Paris-based Station F and London-based Founders Factory, to get first dibs on the start-ups that compete for access each year. Every year, the open innovation team supports twenty or more high-potential entrepreneurs to whom it offers strategic and operational advice, and, as in the case of Tailify, a chance to partner on joint projects. Another way in which L'Oréal feeds its ecosystem is through equity investments, most recently through its own BOLD (Business Opportunities for L'Oréal Development) fund and in China through a partnership with Cathay Innovation, a Chinese venture capital fund.

The importance and impact of the ecosystem in continuing L'Oréal's legacy of outside-in learning is evident. Beyond the technology associated with many of their start-ups, enthusiastic entrepreneurs have their finger on the pulse of today's and tomorrow's consumers and their needs, ranging from personalized beauty solutions to environmental and societal concerns, cultural specificities, and more. One exciting example is that of Poietis, a young biotech company that designs human biological tissues for research and regenerative medical applications. Poietis and L'Oréal researchers are working together on developing the technology to bio-print hair follicles. One can imagine an endless range of applications, including hair loss treatment but also shampoos and hair color, potentially creating worthy twenty-first-century heirs to Eugène Schueller's early 1900s hair dyes.

Omnichannel Partnerships

L'Oréal's entry into the world of retail is recent. In-store sales still represent a small percentage of global sales, mostly through branded stores such as Kiehl's and, more recently, Lancôme. E-commerce through the company's own branded platforms skyrocketed during the COVID-19 pandemic, having previously grown at a steady pace. Most of the group's sales are made through retailers, whether online or offline, with no direct consumer access for L'Oréal. One of the main challenges for brands that do not have direct access to consumers is the collection of consumer data from each transaction. The equation is a simple but dire one that can easily spell the demise of big non-retail brands: no direct access to consumers equals no direct access to their data, which means reduced targeting and customer engagement.

Hence the need for strategic partnerships that boost access to consumers and at the same time guarantee access to their data. Over the past several years, L'Oréal has built tremendous competitive advantage and market leadership by entering early into partnerships with the giant Chinese platforms Alibaba, Tencent, and Baidu, offering these companies access to L'Oréal's enviable brand portfolios in exchange for preferred access to desirable data. These partnerships also foster innovative solutions such as a voice-activated app on Baidu that allows consumers to access a hands-free hair coloring tutorial. No more product smudges on your phone screen!

L'Oréal has also built a sizable presence on Boutiqaat, a multi-brand Middle Eastern platform where influencer marketing and retail come together. Consumers benefit from the advice of some 200 influencers, each with their own boutique, who recommend products to their customers.

Combining offline and online, Hong Kong–based A.S. Watson, the world's largest international health and beauty retailer with 15,000 stores across twenty-five countries, lets customers virtually try on a wide range of L'Oréal Paris and Maybelline makeup products using a ModiFace-powered app, and delivers the shopper's selected products to their home or their local Watson's store. The greater the integration between technology, product, and retail, the greater the quantity and quality of data that can be collected and the greater the value for the two partners.

Professional Partnerships

As far back as the 1930s, L'Oréal organized training seminars for hair stylists and colorists. In the 1960s, one hundred or so professionals a week would participate in L'Oréal-sponsored Technical Study Days to learn how to use the latest products with their customers. An internal 1967 memo captured this strategy: "Hairdressers are professional artisans who must be able to perform as artists as well as competent technicians to meet the needs of more demanding, better informed, free-willed customers."

Fifty years later, the same strategy drives initiatives to support the digital transformation of the hair care profession. In early January 2020, L'Oréal welcomed the first students of its Hairdressing and Entrepreneurship bachelor's degree, a program that combines technical mastery with multidisciplinary skills in entrepreneurship and digital technology. The idea is to enable hair professionals to actively manage and optimize their customers' hair care and beauty journeys in partnership with the brands they choose to represent. This initiative comes on the heels of the 2019 launch in France of *Top Stylist, a* competition modeled after the famous *Top Chef* culinary competition, to select the ten hair care entrepreneurs with the most compelling business plans. Candidates are selected on their artistic merits and technical qualities as well as their entrepreneurial aptitudes. The ten finalists get to spend six months at the Station F incubator, working on the launch of their start-up, with the support of entrepreneurship coaches and L'Oréal professionals. L'Oréal is progressively transforming the professional hair care ecosystem for the digital era, all the while reinforcing its ties to the profession and ensuring greater access to consumer data and insights.

In the skin care business, L'Oréal has forged similar partnerships with the medical profession, such as with dermatologists and cosmetic surgeons who prescribe specialty products for issues such as acne and eczema, and, increasingly, for sun protection. Across sectors, categories, and brands, human conversations take place daily between L'Oréal employees and the professionals who recommend, use, and sell its products. These conversations serve many purposes: beyond strengthening commercial ties; they educate L'Oréal partners on the latest products and features, and they provide some of the most powerful data any brand could want to get its hands on, the qualitative, firsthand, practical, real-life experience of professionals who interact with consumers day in and day out and know their needs, anxieties, and happy moments.

******

We've seen throughout this chapter how listening and learning practices that developed as early as L'Oréal's first couple of decades have not only been preserved but continue to drive many of the most important current strategies. Many of these listening practices have been turned into preemptive competitive advantage, as is the case with the very strong, often exclusive ties to the hair care profession across most markets.

We have also begun to see how these practices are being translated into the digital world, often becoming digitally enabled, always being used to weave stronger relationships with business partners and consumers. These "translations" do not happen without triggering significant issues, particularly pertaining to data privacy, and we will discuss how L'Oréal addresses them in later chapters. But the legacy of these listening and learning practices gives the company tremendous power within the group. Whether the information flows from a face-to-face conversation or the accessing of a customer's clickstream, listening practices at L'Oréal have always been driven by sheer curiosity, the curiosity that allows you to better understand your customers so you can deliver a more relevant solution to meet their needs. Politeness of the heart is still present in L'Oréal's corporate culture.

TRANSFORMATION TIPS

- Practice listening with curiosity and seek out learning opportunities, and encourage others to do so.
- Favor one-to-one human conversations that support politeness of the heart and empathy.
- Nurture your company's capacity to identify trends and key players.
- Expand your company's ability to acknowledge and accept otherness and to share knowledge. Increase your capacity to integrate newcomers, including new brands, without diluting what makes them special, incorporating "others" into your identity.
- Acquire external competencies, evaluating potential acquisitions for the valuable knowledge they will contribute.
- Make human interactions the core of your learning organization.

A Human-Centered Transformation

In Part I, we identified and analyzed the four foundational pillars that underlie L'Oréal's success over the course of its long history: orchestrate creativity, cultivate healthy doubt, learn and innovate with rigor, and listen with curiosity. In Part II, we'll consider how these four pillars have supported the dramatic transformation of the company. Digital transformation is about enabling consumers to take advantage of digital tools to make their relationships with others and with brands more effective and rewarding.

Technology is at the service of people and not the other way around. The required transformation is not about using new tools, it's about changing the way we relate to the world around us, and particularly to other people. For companies, it's about reinventing their role in these new relationships. Rethinking their role and how they create value is difficult for brands and the companies that own them. It isn't just about adopting technology or about agility, and it even goes beyond adopting new business models; the transformation is about being able to make the intellectual and emotional leap, both individually and collectively, to the view that everything your company does is in the service of your customers. This is a difficult step for organizations and for the individuals within them. And it is, of course, where a combination of strong leadership and a culture that supports change and risk taking makes a difference.

In Chapters 5 and 6 we'll look at what digital transformation means for the relationships between customers and brands, as well as among customers. We'll then go on in Chapter 7 to a broader perspective by looking at how digital transformation impacts partnerships, whether these are with suppliers, distributors, retailers, or others. Finally, we will explore the organizational implications of digital transformation in Chapter 8.

CENTERING CUSTOMERS

Imagine a free virtual consultation with a dermatological expert that delivers a precise, personalized skin diagnosis and a list of recommended products, all in a matter of minutes, from the comfort of your own home. This is what users discovering the L'Oréal Vichy brand's skin diagnostic tool SkinConsult AI experienced when it was first introduced in 2019. Online reviewers of the tool thought it was both exciting and a bit daunting. Among them, editors from various beauty magazines and blogs confessed to having been slightly intimidated by receiving a scientific diagnosis through their mobile phones. Most were impressed not just with the diagnosis, but with the personalized regimen recommendation that came with it. While some confide that they would rather have received their assessment in less clinical, more nuanced language, most appreciated the rigor of the analysis. Some reviewers compared SkinConsult favorably to its several close competitors on the market, noting the benefits of having dermatologists involved in the diagnosis.

The launch of SkinConsult AI has been an important moment in the digital transformation of the Vichy brand. Named after the eponymous spa town and mineral water, Vichy was founded in 1931 by a medical doctor and has always stood for scientific rigor. For L'Oréal, Vichy provided a respected clinical label for this first venture into AI-driven skin diagnosis, developed by the ModiFace unit it acquired in 2018. Using machine learning, the algorithm was tested using huge photo databases of real subjects, across ethnicities and skin types. Dermatologists were involved in every step of the development of the diagnosis protocols. The results? Significant upticks in engagement, brand awareness, and conversion rates for Vichy products.

Every aspect of the way SkinConsult was developed and brought to market reflects the radical changes in the relationships between brands and consumers brought about by the internet over the past two decades. The changes can be summed up in one short phrase: the user is in charge. As the internet allowed consumers to find and exchange direct information about what they were buying, and to influence one another, they assumed greater control of their relationship with brands.

The pressure on brands to put customers first increased enough to trigger a wholesale transformation of the markets for consumer goods and services. Consumers seeking a better fit between their needs and the brands and products they use want a say in every facet of these markets, from development to sourcing and manufacturing, to communications, branding, distribution, and, of course, their own consumption experience. Brands respond by leveraging digital technology to get to know their customers intimately and by offering more and more targeted, personalized, and relevant products, services, and experiences. Digital technology acts as an enabler and enhancer throughout these complex interactions and relationships. The mechanism has been described as collaborative or co-creative, but make no mistake about who calls the shots.

As the balance of power began shifting toward consumers, some companies—like L'Oréal—began to understand that customer engagement in all aspects of their journey would become a significant source of value, an opportunity that would require a profound transformation in order to be fulfilled. The companies that remained skeptical, unwilling, or unable to conduct a broad enough change are now left struggling. It is this understanding that is at the core of a successful digital transformation—the clear vision that the opportunity lies in inviting customers into a better, more valuable experience by engaging with them every step of the way, in response to their demands for greater access and transparency. A more valuable experience for consumers results in greater demand and higher willingness to pay, generating greater profits for the brands.

The COVID-19 crisis in early 2020 dramatized what many companies had come to understand in recent years: when it comes to whether or when to undertake digital transformation, companies have never really had a choice. In a context of lockdowns and restrictions, consumers were looking to engage with their favorite brands in a way that felt safe and reassuring. Brands that could oblige reaped the benefits. Companies such as L'Oréal that had advanced significantly in their transformation adapted quickly to lockdown conditions and gained market share and engagement as a result. In effect, the COVID crisis accelerated digital transformation in the most unexpected way.

A Focus Shift

Perhaps the best indication of things to come appeared long before anyone even began talking about digital transformation. It was the shift, at first subtle and then more dramatic, in how companies and brands think about their customers, gradually increasing their focus on customer service and customer experience. Most companies, L'Oréal included, functioned in a product-centric manner through the late 1990s, and some well into the early 2000s. This meant that they were organized along product lines and were product-driven in their strategy. More recently, many of these companies have shifted toward customer centricity. Rather than pushing products to market, they have reversed their approach to put the primary emphasis on fulfilling their customers' needs, getting their customers' "jobs done."[1] Consumers' "jobs-to-be-done" are the problems they are trying to solve in their lives, the jobs they get products or services to perform for them. Some are practical and focused, such as finding a new lipstick that doesn't smudge to wear for work, while others are broader and less concrete, often emotional, such as feeling better about the image you project on screen when you are on a Zoom call.

The all-important customer journey becomes the roadmap that guides everything a brand does. The implications of this approach range from strategic to organizational to operational and marketing-related. Two forces coincided in time to drive this dramatic change. One was the internet and the reversal of the old-order information asymmetry between brands and customers. Brands know much more about the products they sell than they are willing to tell consumers. It is this asymmetry that is increasingly being called into question by consumers who will no longer settle for anything less than full disclosure. The second force, independent of the first, is increased consumer skepticism toward big brands following scandals and concerns involving child labor, unsafe or unethical testing, deceptive labeling, and more. More generally, as consumers have become more concerned about issues related to the environment, diversity and inclusion, and political choices, their skepticism and frustration toward brands whose projected values do not align with their own has grown. Consumer behavior research suggests that as consumers are exposed to more sophisticated persuasion tactics, they develop greater resistance or "coping" mechanisms, which in turn leads to more persuasive attempts.[2]

As skeptical consumers asked more questions, they were also able to get more answers via the internet. As part of their coping mechanisms, consumers began to trust one another more than they do the brands themselves. Gone is the era of one-way marketing where brands control the messaging and choose when, where, and how it is delivered. Today, brands need to work hard at understanding their customers' journeys, and these have become more unpredictable, social, and personal. Achieving customer engagement and satisfaction requires that companies acknowledge that most touchpoints along these journeys are not initiated or controlled by brands but by customers themselves or people they trust.

Some companies have turned customer centricity into a quasi-cult. Enter Tony Hsieh, the late CEO of Zappos, the online shoe retailer who turned what could have been a business model no-no—selling shoes online, a venue that didn't provide a chance to try them on—into a winning proposition. Can't try the shoes on in a store? How about trying them on in the comfort of your own home and sending them back for free if you don't like them? Can't get a salesperson's advice? How about calling us for a consultation and friendly chat? Can't find the right color match? How about we find it for you, even if it means getting them from our competitors? In the company's early years, as Zappos sought to expand beyond its Bay Area facilities, Hsieh was looking for new headquarters. He and his leadership team settled on Las Vegas for its highly service-oriented workforce trained in the hospitality industry. Every decision is customer driven. Behind the success of Zappos and Hsieh's customer-centric philosophy lies the realization that the retail model for buying shoes was no longer fit-for-purpose, as customers were looking for a broader choice and a better experience.

For the developers of SkinConsult AI, the work also started with understanding customer pain points: hard-to-get doctors' appointments, intrusive and expensive tests, the embarrassment of a skin flaw, the hard sell at the beauty counter, the guilt of having bought too many products.

From there, it was about developing a simple three-minute self-guided diagnostic test that users can go through on their own device: private, precise, relevant, personalized, real-time accessible, trustworthy, reliable, conversational, shareable. Beyond resolving user pain points, SkinConsult delivers value in many ways for Vichy. Every user who uploads her picture and answers questions or subsequently interacts with the brand provides data that enriches Vichy's understanding of skin types and features by geography, climate, and more, and, of course, opens up a conversation with that consumer.

Launching conversations that create engagement and enable personalization is key to customer centricity. Tapping into predigital practices, Zappos encourages its customers to call and chat with its customer representatives on topics ranging from fit and color to occasion appropriateness and more. In a tech-enabled world, this conversational opportunity translated for L'Oréal into Beauty Gifter, a chatbot that enables personalized conversations with customers on Facebook Messenger. Conversations add an extra layer of engagement to the virtual makeup try-on that has now become standard for most brands. Brands ranging from mass distribution like Maybelline and NYX all the way to luxury such as YSL and Shu Uemura have made virtual try-on ubiquitous on social media as part of a partnership with Facebook.

Behind all the bells and whistles of apps and bots, customer centricity hasn't come easily for most companies, L'Oréal included, and many vestiges of product-centric thinking remain, often in the mindsets of leaders and managers. And mindsets are notoriously difficult to shift. Until recently, many business schools continued to instill a product-centric mindset in their students, churning out generation upon generation of managers lacking customer-centric skills and conviction. From an individual perspective, executives who have built successful careers in a product-centric environment find it hard to shift to customer-first thinking. At the corporate level, the old adage of "If it ain't broke, don't fix it" often operates. Many companies have "ticked the box" of digital transformation without having undergone the massive collective and individual mindset shift that is required. Often, digitization is an added layer that sits atop an organization that remains profoundly product-centric.

This is where L'Oréal's cultural legacy has made a difference. Together, the four pillars we've identified—orchestrate creativity, cultivate healthy doubt, learn and innovate with rigor, and listen with curiosity—support a culture in which change is welcome and positive rather than threatening and resisted and where risk-taking is encouraged. There is clear consistency and alignment between the cultural legacy, the leadership's discourse and strategy, and the actions taken across the company by individual teams launching customer-centric and digital solutions. Within any corporate transformation, there comes a point for each individual where change becomes a personal matter of challenging what you had taken for granted. As they reached this moment, managers and leaders found that the hard work they had to perform, of challenging their most deeply engrained business beliefs and assumptions, was supported, encouraged, and recognized within the prevailing culture.

One such leader is Stéphane Bérubé, L'Oréal CMO for Western Europe. Bérubé joined L'Oréal in 2002, as the company was on the cusp of understanding the implications of digital technology. His own awakening came in 2014, as CMO of L'Oréal Canada, in a meeting with executive committee members from whom he expected a pat on the back after one of the best years ever for L'Oréal. Instead he was told that "we are doing a terrible job and need to rethink everything we are doing."[3] He calls that moment one of the most valuable lessons he's ever learned.

As part of this awakening, Bérubé realized that simply selling products as the company had been doing for 110 years would no longer make it successful.[4] L'Oréal needed services that would deliver dynamic customer experiences, services like virtual try-on, skin diagnostics, and personalized shades of foundation. Approaching customers from the perspective of their experience with a product, a service, or a brand provides a holistic perspective on the customer, one in which each customer's "jobs-to-be-done" and pain points become the brand's problem to solve and should preoccupy every manager. Back in the 1950s, under the leadership of François Dalle, L'Oréal and its mass-market shampoo brand Dop addressed a significant postwar customer problem: poor hygiene practices. They launched the "clean children's crusade" to promote greater cleanliness across France. Vans stopped in every major city, distributing soap and shampoo in schools and after-school programs and encouraging teachers to teach basic hygiene practices.

In the same way that Dop vans traveled to meet children and their teachers on their own turf, consumer-centric brands work on being reachable by their customers "anytime, anywhere." Not only can a conversation be struck up on any social network, it can seamlessly take the customer all the way to the checkout screen as boundaries between social platforms and transactional platforms disappear. Again, the customer journey becomes the roadmap.

We characterized digital transformation as a profound change in the way companies think of their customers; it should therefore come as no surprise that we see personalization as an important aspect of digital transformation. Guive Balooch, Global Vice President in charge of the Tech Incubator, puts it this way: "Customers are looking for products designed just for them, with ingredients tailored to their skin type, environment or individual desires. New digital technologies bring the era of hyper-customized cosmetics, a paradigm shift for companies. We must make hyper-personalization the new mass model."[5]

Lancôme launched its personalized face foundation Le Teint Particulier in 2016. The foundation is blended and dispensed on demand in-store from a device the size of a coffee machine within about twenty minutes. Now, Lancôme is developing the capacity to produce customized foundation at scale in its own plants with a range of 22,000 shades. Machinery that can produce tiny batches of thirty milligrams one right after the other is being tested in China for future deployment in L'Oréal plants throughout the world, a big departure from the usual 500-kilogram batches of individual colors typically produced.

Underlying this manufacturing challenge and the technology behind it is the very "job" that foundation "does" for a Lancôme consumer. For many customers, the product is about being confident that your skin feels natural and looks its best. Most foundation users would probably agree that the search for a natural-looking color match can be fraught with frustration and results in many half-used tubes and pots sitting in bathroom cabinets. Knowing that a product has been made just for you is a sure remedy to this frustration, a certain confidence booster.

The team in charge of running the development of Le Teint Particulier took on the challenge of reimagining the experience of buying and wearing foundation. They benefited from the stories of decades of people before them who had imagined new solutions, defied conventional wisdom, tried new things and succeeded, tried other new things and failed, spent afternoons chatting with consumers at the makeup counter, and stood up to their bosses and colleagues. This is what digital transformation is made of: one transformational project after another, informed by talking to your customers, driven by a real desire to invent new solutions, empowered by and integrated into a bigger strategy, stimulated and encouraged by an organization whose culture is to dream big and make risk-taking fathomable and exciting. The artificial intelligence and other technological elements behind it? They are the means to an end; they are there to be fashioned into creative solutions by consumer-driven visionaries.

Precision Marketing

Ask the leaders of any company who in their organization is driving their digital transformation and you will get a different answer from each. Whether it's IT, strategy, or operations, leaders are often convinced that they are the one who is making it happen. At L'Oréal, alongside the innovation units driving the development of new solutions, the HR teams leading the upskilling, recruitment, and organizational challenges, and all the other transformed functions, marketing is very much at the forefront of the transformation. How could it be otherwise, if striking up conversations with your customers is your first preoccupation?

One issue that has arisen for marketers as they have embraced digital transformation is what to call their domain. Referring to their craft as digital marketing suggests that there is another kind of marketing that is not digital marketing. Clearly not an option: marketing is digital through and through. As technology and artificial intelligence have made their mark on the marketing function, and in particular on the way advertising is sold and delivered to customers, the term *programmatic marketing* has been used. It refers to the real-time matching of a marketer's message and target audience with actual customers for whom the message, how and when it's being delivered (or "served," in marketing parlance), has been determined algorithmically to be relevant. While useful, the term remains technical and fails to reflect customer centricity.

L'Oréal has adopted the term *precision marketing* to capture its efforts to use digital technology to identify and engage precisely with customers. The precision is in the targeting, but more importantly it is in the relevance that each interaction brings to a customer. It is as much about knowing when to shut up as when to speak up. CDO Lubomira Rochet refers to it as moving from "cookie-based" marketing (based on the bits of code capturing each user's preferences that make targeting more accurate) to "people-based marketing."[6] This has meant a reorganization of the marketing function to integrate communications with previously siloed digital expertise as well as previously outsourced domains such as media buying. Bérubé puts it this way: "I don't want a digital manager— I want a precision marketing specialist. I want an audience manager. I want a community manager." Crucially, the precision element in precision marketing also refers to the ability to measure performance in the most rigorous way possible. Precise targeting and messaging lead to high levels of relevance for customers, which in turn drives performance against objectives such as engagement and sales, measured relentlessly for continuous optimization. François Dalle's "do, undo, redo" mantra still echoes in this test-and-learn optimization approach.

In the new precision marketing organization, specific projects are organized around touchpoints in the customer journey and bring together the experts who can make things happen. Again, the words of François Dalle resonate: "Advertising is a profession of listening that must always prioritize our respect for consumers,"[7] as does the legendary story of Lindsay Owen-Jones striking up conversations with Japanese consumers on the streets of Tokyo and being invited to follow them to their hair salons.

Seamless Customer Journeys

In early December 2019, Lancôme inaugurated La Maison du Bonheur, the House of Happiness, its first flagship store in Paris, on the Champs Elysées. The 3,000-square-foot boutique has been designed as an innovative experiential space, immersing guests in the world of the luxury brand from the moment they set foot in the store. The rose symbol, the brand's logo for its entire history, is used throughout the store. A "Rose Robot" allows customers to use a robotic arm to choose their own rose, which is then used to personalize all their purchases. Tech meets tradition and brand authenticity. Everything is done to strike up engagement and conversation, both tech-mediated and with beauty advisors.

The brick-and-mortar flagship is part of an omnichannel strategy in which different channels are integrated around the customer journey, each touchpoint offering its distinctive opportunity for engagement and reinforcing the overall seamless experience. Beyond promoting engagement, the function of the flagship store is to have a halo effect across channels by embodying the essence of the brand.

For Lancôme, the opening of its flagship store also signifies a highly visible entry into the world of direct-to-consumer distribution (DTC) for a brand that has traditionally only been sold in multi-brand department stores or beauty retailers like Sephora. Lancôme's distribution model is characteristic of most L'Oréal brands. Unlike many of its competitors, L'Oréal has few DTC brands; having sold its ill-fated Body Shop brand and stores to Brazil's Natura, its main retail brand is Kiehl's. The foray into DTC represents a chance to exert greater control over an important customer touchpoint and gain better insights into part of their customers' journey.

Conversion Across Channels

When it comes to creating engagement and driving consumers to conversion (conversion from consideration to purchase), the retailer's holy grail, seamlessness is the name of the game. Any hiccup or gap in the customer's journey means a missed opportunity to continue the conversation and a possibility they will slip away into a competitor's more compelling world. Customer journey management is an important aspect of marketing, one that makes great use of digital and tech tools. Tracking customers' journeys with a view to managing them seamlessly and optimally requires both data analysis expertise and excellent customer empathy. It is about gaining such intimate knowledge of your customers through their every search, visit, click, and order that the reality of their experience becomes yours to fulfill by using any number of communication and omnichannel tools, both physical and digital.

One such digital asset is ModiFace, the technology subsidiary behind a number of artificial intelligence (AI) and augmented reality (AR) services developed in recent years. AR mobile apps such as try-on and in-store magic mirrors not only enhance the customer experience but serve as conversion tools as they create a seamless experience from consideration to purchase whether in-store or online.

Garnier's virtual hair color try-on, Color Match, reached a record million downloads in Brazil in a matter of a few months. In a prime example of seamlessness, consumers can use the feature anywhere Garnier hair color brands Olia and Nutrisse are sold simply by pointing their phone camera at the product shelves. The result? Conversion rates tripled.

As a consequence of the COVID-19 pandemic and greater focus on sanitary precautions, virtual try-ons are certain to become as ubiquitous in brick-and-mortars as they are online, making omnichannel experiences even more consistent for any given brand.

Brick-and-mortar retailers forced to compete with e-commerce have adopted many of the best practices of e-retailers and become more sophisticated in continuously evaluating the performance of their resources, from real estate to sales advisors to data. Key online performance indicators such as browsing time, unique visitors, abandoned carts, and conversion rates have now been integrated into the dashboards available to brick-and-mortar managers. With more indicators at their disposal comes the opportunity for multi-brand retailers to improve performance by working more collaboratively and effectively with the brands they carry, another important area for L'Oréal's precision marketers, who must manage key physical touchpoints for greater engagement, in line with the company's test-and-learn and rigorous learning tradition.

Integrated Consumer Experience

Much of the challenge for L'Oréal brands in developing omnichannel strategies has been their reliance on retailers, whether online or offline, for both distribution and data collection. An integrated, seamless experience is far more difficult to deliver for brands that do not have their own distribution and retail channels, or access to consumer data. The intricate and fast-changing ecosystem of online and offline retailers adds a dose of complexity to partnership options. From a customer perspective, seamlessness is about the convenience of a store near her, or a buy button on whatever platform she happens to be visiting—whether it is the brand's own site, an e-commerce app, a consumer-to-consumer platform, or social media. Building partnerships within this ecosystem requires a keen understanding of its dynamics and of consumer preferences.

Stephane Rinderknech, former CEO of L'Oréal China, now heading up U.S. operations, recounted the calculated gamble he took back in 2012 upon agreeing to the condition set by Tmall CEO Daniel Zhang that he feature all of the company's luxury brands on the then-fledgling platform. The gamble paid off in a huge way, as L'Oréal's partnership with Tmall is now a significant part of the company's success story in China, featuring among its top-selling brands throughout the year and on notorious shopping festivals such as Singles' Day. Rinderknech credited the decentralized decision-making structure and culture at L'Oréal, an approach we have referred to as "Go Forth and Innovate," with empowering him to make a split-second decision when Zhang presented him with the Tmall deal.

Another Asia-based retail juggernaut, Hong Kong–based A.S. Watson (ASW), operates more than 15,000 stores in twenty-five countries. The retailer is present in Asia under the Watsons brand, in Europe under Marionnaud, and in the United Kingdom as Superdrug. L'Oréal and ASW have built a strong partnership based in large part on their drive to innovate together. In early 2019, they co-launched #ColourMe, a virtual makeup try-on service on Watsons' mobile applications in Asia, based on L'Oréal's ModiFace technology. As users are trying on any of the hundreds of makeup products available, they can create and save their own looks, record their try-ons, and then go straight to the buy button for home delivery or in-store pickup in four hours.

This seamless omnichannel vision was at the heart of L'Oréal's acquisition of Korean beauty brand Stylenanda in 2018. K-beauty, as South Korean beauty products are known, has been at the forefront of innovative worldwide distribution models. As the craze for K-beauty products reached the United States and other Western markets, consumers themselves drove innovation by inventing their own access to the products before the goods were even distributed in their markets. They developed a hands-on approach to sourcing and using the products to suit their individual needs.

Amazon first made the products available, followed by Sephora, who took an early lead. This consumer-driven market expansion process means that K-beauty brands, including Stylenanda, are perfectly attuned to their consumers' jobs-to-be-done both in terms of the products themselves and in terms of how to make them available. The brand has a highly visible presence on social media, on e-commerce platforms, in multi-brand stores, and with its own unique flagship stores, including the Seoul-based six-story Stylenanda Pink Hotel, offering wildly creative on-brand experiences with its evocative over-the-top lobby, laundry room, and pool levels. Each floor provides a unique immersion experience, a highly Instagrammable story for shoppers to tell their friends, a compelling conversation starter for any K-beauty aficionada worth her donkey milk sheet mask.

The Strategic Use of Data

Evidence-based decision making has been part of L'Oréal's culture for decades. Eugène Schueller insisted on talking to the women who bought his hair dyes and the pharmacists who sold them so he could understand their needs. François Dalle's visit to a New York–area drugstore helped him understand the U.S. hair color market. Stories abound of Lindsay Owen-Jones sitting at the wheel of a Russian delivery truck, driving an East German Trabant, or walking through the streets of Bombay or Tokyo. The deeply engrained test-and-learn culture is also based on a strong respect for data and evidence. Digital transformation has brought with it tremendous opportunities to collect, extract, store, share, and process data.

Consumer Insights Drive Innovation

One of the areas in which the early partnership between L'Oréal and Alibaba's Tmall has paid off is in the sharing of consumer data to enable research and innovation. In 2018, Alibaba had more than half a billion consumers. On average, each opened their shopping app eight times a day and spent thirty minutes discovering, sharing, and buying new products. Vast quantities of rich data are collected using these consumers' clickstreams as they make their way along the customer journey from search to consideration, purchase, post-purchase, and repeat. Unlike other global e-commerce players such as Amazon, Tmall has a strategy of sharing data with brands in order to facilitate collaborative innovation.

In 2018, Tmall and L'Oréal partnered on a project to make significant inroads into the growing Chinese male grooming market. They accessed Tmall-generated search and clickstream data to understand male consumers' jobs-to-be-done and turn them into new products and solutions. Having identified five different segments reflecting grooming preferences and lifestyles, the two companies launched an integrated campaign targeting consumers in each of the five segments. Male consumers visiting a co-branded Hangzhou pop-up store to celebrate the launch in China of David Beckham's House 99 brand were invited to experience one of five showrooms reflecting their preferred style. In addition to promoting the brand, starting conversations, and driving engagement, marketers used the event as an opportunity to observe consumers in the flesh and develop richer qualitative insights that will allow them to craft more relevant offers.

Business Insights Drive Performance

Among the challenges that L'Oréal and most other companies leading a digital transformation have had to face is how to manage the sheer quantity of data in a way that makes it available to anyone across the organization who needs access either to the raw data or, more critically, to the analytics that can be extracted. Finding an appropriate solution between full centralization that allows standardization and economies of scale and full autonomy of individual units in managing their data is a real challenge for large companies, particularly ones with a decentralized structure, like L'Oréal.

Another significant issue for L'Oréal, as for other large marketing organizations, is the question of data privacy. As more data is collected and extracted, consumers, watchdog groups, and policy makers have increasing and justified concerns about companies' and governments' use of data and the potential for abuse.

Recent cases such as the 2018 Cambridge Analytica scandal, in which consumer data extracted from up to 87 million Facebook profiles was found to have been used to target specific voters in advance of the 2016 U.S. presidential elections and, allegedly, the Brexit referendum,[8] have only served to increase these concerns.

While European regulators took an early lead in requiring greater transparency on the part of online marketers by giving consumers an explicit choice to accept or reject cookies (through the 2018 GDPR [General Data Protection Regulation]), convenience and practicality make the reject option almost useless. In the United States, there is little federal regulation, leaving any potential effort to state legislators.

Consumers around the world vary greatly in how willing they are to share data; Chinese consumers are notoriously more open to sharing their personal data than their Western counterparts. The difficulty for marketers is in finding the appropriately ethical cost-benefit balance between privacy infringement and delivering extra relevance to consumers in the form of better targeted offers. Emmanuel Lulin, L'Oréal's Chief Ethics Officer since 2007, recently commented on this and other corporate ethical challenges in a tech-enabled context: "I think the key criteria to distinguish a slightly more ethical organization from a slightly less ethical organization is . . . the sincerity with which we walk the talk. It's not compliance, because compliance just asks us to obey.... Ethics is not about obeying—it's about agreeing."[9] In addition to Lulin's role, and to reflect its decentralized structure, L'Oréal has a team of seventy-five "ethics correspondents" throughout the world, employees from across the company's functions who work with the executive committee and their country managers to encourage ethical practices.

Beyond extracting consumer insights for innovation, consumer clickstreams can also be used to analyze the efficiency of marketing efforts. Key performance indicators such as return on investment, share of voice in a given market or a given media, conversion rates for certain types of messages or media, and many others can be calculated and used as business insights to continuously optimize marketing actions. In recent years, as the quantities of data grew exponentially and the urgency to extract business insights from the data accelerated, executives at L'Oréal acknowledged that existing solutions were both too slow and too fragmented. Former Global Chief Data Officer Vincent Stuhlen spearheaded the development of an analytics tool, dubbed "cockpit," that puts marketing performance indicators at the disposal of everyone in the organization. Datasets from the entire organization are centralized on the platform, processed and governed centrally. Individual business units are able to inject their own data and have access to their own dashboards. Different types of dashboards are available for operational teams, strategic decision makers, and executive teams. This policy of equal and open access in turn opens up more frequent, natural, and productive performance conversations internally, and results in more effective and timely business decision making.

******

Digital transformation has in many ways been triggered and driven by the evolution of consumer behavior in the digital age, and in particular the increased emphasis on conversations, which a digital organization also supports. The leadership team—starting with CEO Jean-Paul Agon, Chief Digital Officer Lubomira Rochet, and others such as the heads of regions and functional areas—has sought to strike an effective balance between leading the transformation from the top and letting it blossom from the grassroots. They've also been able to count on a strong culture that is aligned with the transformation strategy and favors innovation from the ground up, orchestrated creativity, rigorous learning, and empathetic curiosity toward consumers. These three elements—top-down leadership, grassroots empowerment, and a culture that encourages change and risk-taking—account for much of the success in transforming relationships between L'Oréal brands and their customers.

TRANSFORMATION TIPS

- Make customer centricity the focus of your digital transformation. Rather than selling products, your objective must be to solve your customers' problems, to get their jobs done.

- Innovate to create more value for consumers by better fulfilling their jobs to be done, their pain points and their gain points.

- Develop a state-of-the-art precision marketing machine that takes advantage of data and channels to provide optimal relevance to each customer.

- Introduce product personalization and differentiation as late as possible in the value chain.

- Implement a holistic "journey" approach to customer experience, integrating offline and online touchpoints for a unique and seamless experience for customers.

- Analyze data for insights that help you detect new trends and customize offers for specific consumers or segments.

- Create a company-wide insights engine that enables units (brands and markets) to benefit from one another's data and insights.

- Think of your customers as individuals and treat them with respect and empathy.

BECOMING SOCIAL

M eet Militza Yovanka, a twenty-eight-year-old Serbian social influencer specializing in beauty and fashion. A self-described "makeup lover, fashion passion and body positivity advocate," Yovanka began posting selfies and videos sharing her beauty tips and routines in 2015 and now has 1.1 million followers on Instagram, putting her squarely in the category of macro-influencers. Watching Yovanka's YouTube videos feels like peeking into a one-character "girls' night in" where it's okay to say silly things and let it all out, while you talk about your brow line and how much rocky road ice cream you can eat in one go. Her 2018 nine-minute video called the "Perfect Eyebrow Tutorial" garnered 909,000 views. In the video, Yovanka confides that she ruined her eyebrows by getting a brow tattoo followed by a botched laser treatment. "My brows are not perfect, they are not symmetrical, but that's okay," she shares. In another YouTube video, she creates her own original tie-dye hair look by layering different shades of L'Oréal's Colorista semi-permanent colors. Yovanka, a confident and friendly girl-next-door type, draws you in with a mix of warmth, slight self-deprecation about her less-than-perfect English, and occasional references to the challenges of her earlier life. She doesn't shy away from injecting offbeat and humorous moments. She drops a tube of makeup on the floor and says, "Whoops, just dropped something." No need for a retake. What you see is what you get.[1]

Yovanka's videos cleverly straddle the boundary between her private life and her social and professional life. Beauty as she defines it through her videos is both personal and private, and deeply social. It's about feeling good and confident about yourself, yet projecting an image that meets certain criteria—that "perfect brow" that takes ten minutes to paint onto your face using a mix of brushes, powders, concealers, soap, brow filler, and . . . a razor blade. Yovanka, a L'Oréal influencer, embodies and dramatizes the questions that occupy managers at L'Oréal: How does our increasingly social media–enabled life change the way we think about and practice beauty? As so many of our social interactions with others become tech mediated, and the image we project of ourselves is increasingly captured on screen and shareable, do we need to rethink what makes up this image?

The pervasiveness of social media has precipitated a change in the way we define beauty, in particular the relationship between what we will call personal beauty and social beauty. By personal beauty, we mean our sense of our own beauty. It is linked to what psychologists and marketing scholars call "body image."[2] Because we also include beauty care in our definition of beauty, personal beauty incorporates personal care that enhances our personal beauty without it necessarily being visible to others. This includes skin care products such as cleansers and moisturizers, body care products such as bath oils and lotions, and those for hair care such as conditioners. As consumers' notion of beauty begins to cross over into well-being, personal beauty care can also include products such as scented candles or home fragrances that help us relax and, possibly, feel more beautiful.

Social beauty, on the other hand, is about the image of beauty we intentionally project to others. Psychology and marketing scholars refer to this as self-presentation.[3] Watching Yovanka's videos leaves no doubt that personal and social beauty are interconnected and feed into each other. My sense of my own beauty is influenced by how others see me, and the image of beauty I project to others is shaped by my own beauty judgment. However, the distinction between these two aspects of beauty is important and more and more relevant as technology makes it easier for consumers to manipulate their image both in person and virtually for self-presentation purposes. With the rise of social media, particularly the use of photos and selfies,[4] consumers show increasing interest not just in self-presentation, but also in discussing with others, including influencers like Yovanka, how they fashion the image they project, their social beauty. They do so in tutorials, blogs, and social networks, using a mix of language and visuals including pictures and videos. In the fashion domain, virtual fashion has made its appearance—if you can buy a virtual outfit to wear on Instagram, why bother with the real thing?

Among the many disruptions it has triggered, the COVID-19 crisis has prompted consumers to reconsider how important their beauty routines are in defining their personal and professional image. "I can't pretend like life is just going on as usual when it's not," says Yovanka in an April 2020 video, "but you still have to show your face on Zoom."[5] Consumers have taken to social media to comment on what it's like watching yourself for hours on end on a computer screen. Some look for new screen-friendly makeup tricks to emphasize their eyes, for a more expressive effect. Others opt for a natural, no-makeup look. Similar questions arise about hair care, skin care, and nail care. The crisis has brought to the forefront of consumers' minds a question that has occupied managers at L'Oréal for some time: How does our increasingly digitally enabled life change the way we think about and practice beauty? As so many of our social interactions with others become tech mediated, and the image we project of ourselves is increasingly captured on screen and shareable, do we need to rethink what makes up this image?

To engage with consumers looking for makeup solutions that are adapted to remote work or virtual conditions, several L'Oréal brands have developed augmented reality screen lenses for Zoom calls. If personalizing your background isn't enough, try changing your own look! As work practices adapt to a new reality, the standards for appropriate dress also adapt. Fashion brands specializing in professional apparel such as suits and dress shirts have seen their business plummet overnight. Men's clothier Brooks Brothers, a 202-year-old mainstay of American executive attire, recently filed for bankruptcy. Suddenly, social beauty, the way we manage the image we project to others, is thrown up in the air and who knows what it will look like when it lands? Will we continue to apply makeup directly onto our faces, or will we simply opt for virtual application? What about our own personal sense of beauty?

The spike in sales of mindfulness apps, clean beauty products, candles, and home fragrances suggests that alongside our desire to manage our social beauty sits a deeper need for a more holistic approach to beauty that includes self-care for both our physical and our mental selves. What is the role of a beauty company in understanding and satisfying these multiple dimensions of beauty? For marketers, it is clear that the entire beauty value proposition is transformed, not so much by digital technology as a channel, but by digital as a catalyst for broader social changes, for bringing people together around common challenges, interests, or passions or just to have a chat. Every beauty touchpoint in a customer's journey must be redefined for a digitally mediated life where technology matters, but only inasmuch as it shapes human and social experience.

Social Centricity

The beauty sector provides a compelling case study of how digital technology has transformed not just the relationship between brands and customers but also the relationships between customers and what this means for companies like L'Oréal. Because of the deeply human and social nature of beauty, the sector provides a particularly fertile ground for a rich social ecosystem of consumers and experts to thrive and bloom. In any industry, consumer or business-facing, recognizing the inherent power of customers who share their knowledge and experiences with one another, find solutions for one another, and ultimately influence one another's choices represents both a significant opportunity and a considerable challenge of digital transformation.

Fulfilling this opportunity requires going beyond customer centricity to what we might call *social* centricity: the recognition and enablement of the social fabric that is woven one interaction at a time as consumers share information, support one another, and solve problems for one another. For most companies, this requires a strategically soft touch that carefully and creatively weaves together outsiders' and the brand's own voice through different types of channels and messages.

In marketing parlance, the trichotomy of owned, paid, and earned media captures the relationship between a brand and the different channels through which it voices its messages. Owned media, such as websites and catalogs, allow brands to fully control their messaging and the way the content is promoted and diffused. Paid media offer broad promotion and diffusion of the brand's own content. Earned media, the spontaneous sharing of content by satisfied customers on social media, is the most difficult to obtain and control, but it is highly effective in establishing credibility and authenticity. The typology reflects the tradeoff between control and credibility—credibility increases as control over the messaging and media diminishes, but the once-clear boundaries between the three types of media have become increasingly blurred. Whereas a celebrity post could have once been considered earned, it would now most likely fall within the paid category as influencer marketing, affecting the way customers evaluate its credibility. Many influencers such as Yovanka go out of their way to inject spontaneity into their posts and videos to maintain credibility and authenticity. Sitting as they do on that blurry line between earned and paid media, they manage it painstakingly and adeptly.

In contrast to many of its competitors, L'Oréal's understanding of the power and complexity of social influence strategies goes back to its early days and to the very core of its business: hairdressers have played an important role in influencing their clients to use L'Oréal products for more than a century. They are now given tools to work with their clients remotely and continue their conversations beyond the salon. The Color&Co service matches colorists and clients for one-on-one hair color customization and at-home application.

Digital technology has transformed consumers' social experience of finding and using beauty products in many ways. As they engage with online peers at different points of their customer journeys, consumers, advisors, influencers, and others offer one another solutions to tricky challenges, provide support and guidance in choosing products, comment on try-ons, help each other choose and buy, teach each other how to use new products, and listen to each other talk about what worked and what didn't. These interactions around social beauty can run the gamut from one-time *liking* or commenting to frequent conversations and sharing of selfies or videos. The relationships that underlie these interactions can be more or less close and can either extend to *in real life*, or not. To capture this full range of relationships, we refer to peers who interact on social media and other online venues as *friends*, a broad term that doesn't indicate conventional in-real-life friendship but any kind of online peer-to-peer relationship around a brand, product, or practice. Friends are at the core of social beauty and form complex relationships, often positive and supportive, such as finding solutions, giving advice, shopping together, and more. Yovanka greets her viewers as "loves" and "darlings" and refers to other influencers as her friends.

The negative competitive and sometimes destructive aspects of social media relationships, while beyond the scope of this book, should not be overlooked by beauty brands. Teenagers and young adults in particular are known to be very susceptible to the negative effects of social media, particularly in areas that affect self-esteem such as beauty, body image, and social relationships. Fashion brands' important responsibility in promoting healthy body shapes has been discussed for decades, but the spotlight has yet to be cast on beauty brands' own responsibility to promote positive and inclusive standards and messages either directly or via their influencers.

Friends Find Solutions

Seeing online conversations among consumers confronting the emotional challenge of watching their hair roots turn gray during lockdown, L'Oréal Paris hair care managers knew they could offer a solution and seize an opportunity to promote their products. They needed to provide reassurance that covering gray roots was a routine problem shared by many women. They turned to celebrity spokesperson and actress Eva Longoria to deliver a message in a ninety-second video that straddled paid and earned media. Inviting us into her living room, Longoria showed us her own gray roots and, like any independent YouTuber, demonstrated how she used L'Oréal Paris' Excellence Crème for her own thirty-minute "box" color treatment.

Showing her understanding of consumers' reticence to try the product at home, Longoria reassures them: "Self-care *is* self-worth." While Longoria shot the scenes herself, using her iPhone on a tripod in the style of a YouTube crash test, she was in fact being directed remotely by L'Oréal Paris's creative agency, as for any commercial shoot. The result is a highly engaging, irreverent, and credible piece of advertising (paid) that looks very much like a piece of earned media. With just under a million views on Instagram, the ad garnered a strong response from fans and the blogosphere, hailing a new era of more authentic commercials.

In her video, Longoria channels the average savvy consumer who puts real effort into researching the products she is considering, wanting to make sure they will work for her. Understanding the product—including its ingredients, where it was produced, how to apply it, and what it works for and what it doesn't—occupies an important part of a consumer's engagement with products and brands. In this consideration phase of the customer journey, consumers no longer rely on a brand's word as validation for their purchase. For this, they turn to friends who can share their own experiences with greater authenticity.

Friends Give Advice

Friends ask each other for advice on different looks, share their experience of the benefits and drawbacks of different products, get inspiration from each other, encourage each other to try new styles, and so on. Many consumers also value the advice of influencers or celebrities whom they trust to provide good advice. Heeding recognized experts and siding with likeable individuals are techniques that have helped our ancestors survive over the history of humanity. The success of these techniques at enhancing fitness means that they are very strong motivators of human behavior.

While choosing beauty products is hardly life threatening, it is fraught with dilemmas and uncertainties associated with the image we seek to project to those around us. In fact, throughout the course of history and across cultures, beauty rituals have often possessed a meaningful social dimension. Fashionable seventeenth-century courtesans in France and England sought to impress and influence their friends by entertaining them in their dressing rooms and sharing their "toilette" and makeup rituals, dressed in nothing more than a negligée. Hindu weddings are known for their rich traditions, most of which are performed in the company of family and friends. The Haldi, a blessing ceremony, involves the bride's seven best friends applying a paste of turmeric and oil to her body, proffering both spiritual and physical care. Later the same day, in the Mehndi ceremony, intricate henna designs are painted on the hands and arms of the bride and her party, in a joyful social celebration.

Today, just as in the seventeenth-century boudoirs and the colorful Indian lounges, the substance of consumer conversations around beauty remains the same: they are about confidence, image, influence, fun, care, support, celebration, intimacy, friendship, love, and more. What has changed is that these conversations are now digital and embedded in marketing strategies. In the digital age, channels have become more diverse, audiences have grown exponentially in size and diversity, and the amount of information available is practically unlimited. Marketers have learned to enter these conversations, availing themselves of the richness of information they reflect, their authenticity, and the influence they exert.

As with Eva Longoria's commercial, the blurred boundaries between earned, paid, and owned media make it difficult for consumers to carefully evaluate the true nature of conversations, posts, and other messages. For "indie," celebrity-owned brands such as singer Rihanna's Fenty or media celebrity Kylie Jenner's Kylie, influencer marketing is not just a marketing channel, it is at the core of their business model. For non–"digital native" brands, including most of those in L'Oréal's portfolio, influencer marketing, with all its intricacies and fast-changing rules, comes less naturally and provides a steeper learning curve but constitutes one of the most strategic and effective aspects of their digital transformation.

Friends Take You Places

L'Oréal's acquisition of Urban Decay in 2012 followed by that of NYX Professional Makeup in 2014 marked a double turning point in the company's ability to develop some of the most highly effective influencer marketing strategies. NYX had been built on a shoestring by Korean American entrepreneur Toni Ko, who wanted to translate her own passion for makeup into a simple value proposition that resonated with many consumers: "Department store beauty at drugstore prices."

Having launched NYX in 1999 just as the internet was reaching most U.S. consumers' homes, Ko quickly understood the power of beauty bloggers and influencers, and began sending free samples to social media stars. Her value proposition meant that she needed to reach the mass market quickly, which she was able to accomplish thanks to an early distribution deal with Ulta and later Target. She developed her e-commerce operation early on and watched her business take off until she sold to L'Oréal in 2014 and exited the business.

In addition to a significant mass-market presence, NYX brought L'Oréal its innovative, entrepreneurial, social-first, data-driven, laser-sharp focus on getting their customers' jobs done by selling those customers the products they want at the prices they want to pay. In many ways, knowledge, particularly in the form of how to manage customer centricity, a cutting-edge approach to marketing, and a huge understanding and respect for influencer marketing, was the real prize for L'Oréal in acquiring NYX as L'Oréal sought to tool up in that domain.

Thanks in no small part to NYX, L'Oréal has made tremendous strides in turning itself into an influencer marketing machine that functions across thirty-six brands and 150 countries. Take, for instance, the YSL Beauty Club, a pop-up boutique and nightclub that tours the world with celebrity influencers, including Zoe Kravitz and Edie Campbell. The campaigns are designed at headquarters level, but behind-the-scenes images of events are shared on Instagram with support from local YSL teams in different markets. A recent event was the pop-up Beauty Station at the 2019 Coachella Festival, a retro take on a highway gas station complete with Instagrammable props such as a tour bus, a giant lipstick sign, heart-shaped balloons, convertible cars, and neon-pink gas pumps. The choice of celebrity influencers and the style of the campaign is on-brand with YSL's edgy and subversive brand image of a woman who creates her own rules, reflecting Yves Saint Laurent's own image of the enfant terrible of fashion. While YSL's Coachella experiment generated significant activity on social media, the event functioned more as a traditional PR campaign and launch party for new products than as an influencer engagement campaign, a paid rather than earned media outcome.

The roadshow format is hardly new. In 1952, L'Oréal sponsored a radio song competition that toured the different regions of France. Radio shows at the time could reach up to 75 percent of the national population. Competitors would parade through local towns led by Rodolphe, a little boy who was the official face of Dop shampoo. The shampoo was sold in blister-type packaging similar to that of a traditional small French candy called *berlingot*. Rodolphe sang a jingle that became famous throughout France, "Let me have a berlingot," and the success of the "berlingot Dop" was overwhelming.

Friends Share Their Looks

Influencers such as little Rodolphe can play three possible roles on behalf of brands. They act as endorsers of products and brands, they serve as media channels by sharing content broadly with their fans and followers, and they develop content for brands. In many cases they do all three. The endorsement role, inherited from predigital days, was traditionally played by film or TV stars and models who would bring both their stamp of approval and their glamorous image to brands. Think Andie MacDowell and her many campaigns over thirty years for L'Oréal Paris.

As online social influence became more prevalent and consumers sought to engage in more conversations online, the sharing and content roles of influencers expanded. An influencer sharing content on her channel, whether it's on YouTube, Instagram, or her own platform, blurs the lines between her commercial role on behalf of the brand and her own conversations with fans, or between earned and paid media. When Zoe Kravitz shared her YSL X ZOE KRAVITZ videos on Instagram, she let her 5.8 million followers in on the secret of the new lipstick line she was designing, starting a conversation with them.

As their knowledge of their audience increases, macro influencers can guide brands and their approach. Because they can afford to select the brands with which they work, macro influencers position themselves as curators rather than mouthpieces, thereby retaining some of their credibility. Korean macro influencer Pony defines her role as "a curator and an educator. I work with brands and use their brand story and products to spread makeup artistry around the globe."[6]

An increasing number of brands have also taken to designing special collections with their top influencers, tightening the engagement between the brand, the influencer, and their following. Kristen Leanne, an American advocate of cruelty-free products who has an edgy, badass look and attitude that matches Urban Decay's DNA, launched an eye shadow palette as a collaboration with the brand.

More recently, in their constant quest for greater authenticity and a more natural, "earned" feel, and as they seek to micro-target specific segments more accurately, brands have turned to micro-influencers whose followers are in the thousands rather than the hundreds of thousands or more. As influencer marketing continues to mature and brands increase their investment in the channel, a "spread-your-bets" strategy is emerging of assembling *squads* of influencers with varying follower counts, counting on the macro and mega tiers to drive consumer acquisition, and the micro and nano tiers to engage more deeply with specific consumer niches.

Friends Shop with You

In addition to preventing salon visits, the COVID crisis also kept consumers away from their friends and from stores. For L'Oréal brands and other beauty and fashion labels, the sudden freeze of "in real life" socializing and buying presented a problematic double whammy. Social interactions and shopping are both at the heart of the beauty consumption experience. Not only do we buy cosmetics in large part to improve our look and confidence in social settings, but for many consumers, particularly younger ones, buying is itself a highly social event. Social influence is an important aspect of buying beauty products.

Faced with plummeting sales, beauty marketers in many countries quickly turned to livestreaming, a sales channel that has been embraced by Chinese consumers for several years, rising to phenomenal levels during shopping festivals such as Singles' Day. The $66 billion in Chinese livestreaming sales in 2019 are expected to more than double to $170 billion in 2020, fueled in no small part by the increased demand during China's early lockdown. Soon after most Western markets went into lockdown, many beauty and fashion brands swiftly turned to live commerce and designed celebrity and influencer-led virtual live shopping events, which they streamed on social media and specialist platforms.

These live events bring together consumers, influencers, celebrities, and the brands they love, all just one click away from purchase. Among the L'Oréal brands that experimented with livestreaming during the pandemic lockdown, NYX hosted an all-day live tutorial to celebrate Pride Month 2020, offering free shipping to anyone who tuned in the whole time. Aside from the excitement of exclusive deals, the success of a livestreaming show is directly attributable to the host's influence, as well as to the influence consumers have on one another as they chat together throughout the shows.

Having captured Western beauty shoppers' attention and excitement during the COVID-19 crisis, live commerce is probably here to stay in many markets across the world, a boon for brands and celebrity influencers looking to convert their crowds of social media fans into engaged shoppers. For marketers, livestreaming is a simple way to deliver a seamless experience, all the way from informational, entertaining, and persuasive content to purchase on a single platform. The one-platform acquisition-to-conversion-to-sales channel also means that the data is easily accessible and attributable: acquisition and conversion are mashed up into one quick and highly effective touchpoint thanks to the power of social influence.

Livestreaming is only one of the many new ways of interacting and selling that have emerged as a result of digital transformation; some are brand-mediated, others are not. In most instances, consumers share ideas, tips, and reviews with one another outside of brand-sponsored channels.

Friends Stick Together

By bringing together consumers who share a liking for a brand or have similar hobbies or interests, communities weave a spontaneous and authentic social and cultural fabric around brands. Social media and dedicated community platforms make it possible for consumers to have the conversations that matter to them.

The cosmetics brand Glossier—not a L'Oréal brand—was built around a preexisting community of consumers looking for a natural and healthy look, who felt they had been neglected by so-called big brands and wanted to talk about what mattered to them in their choice of beauty products. Founder Emily Weiss, the "patron saint of dewy skin no makeup makeup"[7] had previously launched and managed *Into the Gloss*, a successful blog that inspired 1.5 million fans who shared tips and supported each other in their search for that more natural look.

Having experimented with social commerce on the blog platform, Weiss saw the potential for a brand that would fulfill her fans' beauty and social needs: a co-created brand that would strengthen the community's social fabric while providing the skin solutions its members were so eager to source. She put it this way in an interview for a Harvard Business School case study: "We're striving not for a breadth of assortment like Amazon, but for a breadth of human connections."[8] This is how Glossier came to life as a community-energized brand of passionate consumers looking as much for a social experience as for skin solutions.

Consumers like Glossier's form communities around a shared purpose. As they contribute to the community, share with each other, and support each other and the brand, the community develops cultural attributes, practices, symbols, and rituals. Fans share their "shelfies" on Instagram, pictures of the top shelf of their bathroom cabinet using the hashtag #itgtopshelfie. Shelfies reveal intimate details about their owners and start authentic conversations. The trust and intimacy that develops among fans who have let each other into their bathrooms is key to the authenticity of the community and, as a result, to its effectiveness in supporting the brand. Fans share tips, review new products, cultivate a sense of belonging, suggest new solutions, encourage each other to try out new looks, invite others to join in, and more. In other words, they perform a job that few good marketers can fill—they bring passion, excitement, and honesty to each other and to the brand, and by doing so attract more people and build greater engagement.

Brands can enter these conversations, but only in the most cautious manner. Any attempt by a brand to exert control or extract value from these communities carries a tremendous risk. This makes community strategies difficult for corporate brands to pull off: the conundrum calls for an "unstrategy" strategy. A quote from Kevin Costner's character in *Field of Dreams* captures the best community strategy: "If you build it, they will come." Brands simply need to provide a compelling (brand) platform and watch the magic happen. Glossier managed to build a successful brand "on top of" its organic community, and to engage its fans in supporting the brand while still preserving much of the community's authenticity. The lesson is that real communities feed off their fans' shared purpose, which must exist beyond the brand's own commercial purpose.

Outside the beauty sector, one of the most successful organic consumer brand communities is the AFOLs (Adult Fans of Lego). The purpose of the AFOL community? For adult fans to share their passion for building with Lego bricks, socialize around their hobby, and express their pent-up creativity. Lego's community engagement strategy provides a good example of the careful, patient, and respectful work that brands should undertake if they are to benefit from the collective power of their fans without threatening the community's authenticity. Building an authentic community remains an elusive target for most corporate brands, as it requires a long-term consumer-centric perspective that is difficult for many brands to combine with short-term business objectives and financial market expectations. *Trust, patience, shared purpose, transparency,* and *co-creation* have yet to catch on in the corporate vocabulary.

******

Customer centricity, we showed in the last chapter, required of L'Oréal a wholesale rethinking of the role of consumers. It amounted to having every part of the organization—every division, every market—invite consumers to step in from the outside and take a seat at the table, and from there, to rethink together everything from strategy to operations. We argued that this rethinking was actually led by consumers, who were demanding a say, leaving little room for hesitancy or delay. We are not underplaying either the challenge or the strategic will that went into this transformation. The social centricity part of the transformation, which we have described in this chapter, has been a more gradual process that was prompted in large part by contextual factors, the development of new technology, and the cultural changes that the technology prompted.

As social networks have added more functionalities like integrated shopping, as bloggers have grown their follower ranks, as data has enabled ever more granular targeting, as indie brands have upped the ante, brands like L'Oréal's have had to constantly challenge themselves to become more and more social-centric, much like a bookish teenager trying to come out of her shell. The challenge has been twofold: on the operational and tech side, there has been a constant need to experiment with new platforms, new functionalities, new knowledge, and new processes, while on the strategic and organizational side, the challenge has been about developing the will to enter into real conversations, accepting the inherent risk of letting unknown twenty-somethings promote your brand to consumers around the world, and learning faster than change can happen. The trick, of course, is keeping the "real" in "real conversations."

The traditional power that legacy brands, such as most of L'Oréal's brands, have amassed and the traditional built-in information asymmetry within legacy companies have made social centricity a remarkably difficult challenge for which any rulebook is old before it's even written. In this, the combination of the four pillars of orchestrate creativity, cultivate healthy doubt, learn and innovate with rigor, and listen with curiosity has served L'Oréal well. The decentralized yet determinedly coordinated organization, which allows innovation to flow from the bottom up as much as from the top down; the challenger mindset that acknowledges opportunities for improvement and favors winning from behind; the relentless and rigorous testing-and-learning; and the curiosity toward the market and consumers have all contributed to L'Oréal's great strides in turning itself and its brands toward social centricity.

TRANSFORMATION TIPS

- Create compelling platforms and content that support relationships between customers, allowing them to get their jobs done by sharing and reacting to content, engaging in conversations, and supporting one another.
- Implement social listening tools to identify and respond to insights, including pain points and service issues.
- Move beyond promoting products on social networks to creating strong relationships with communities, a key point to boosting engagement.
- Develop launch strategies that allow consumers to promote new products.
- Develop platforms that encourage consumers to review, like, and share your products and services.
- Design numerous opportunities for consumers to interact with experts and get advice.
- Develop a multifaceted influencer strategy by identifying and developing in-depth relationships with key influencers.
- Integrate your influencer strategy into your marketing and social strategy, using your customers' journeys as your guide.
- Don't overlook the emergence of micro-influencers, who have close ties with their communities and can become remarkable assets. A team of micro-influencers can play a key role in boosting your brands across social networks.
- Be ready to lose some control as consumers become your advocates; respect their advocacy.
- Social interactions are at the core of value creation and must be privileged.

TRANSFORMING RELATIONSHIPS WITH PARTNERS

For Southeast Asian beauty consumers coming out of their post-COVID-19 lockdown in June 2020, "Back to Beauty," a three-day livestreaming event hosted by L'Oréal and e-commerce platform Lazada, offered a welcome chance to get tips on keeping their skin blemish-free while wearing a mask and, more generally, how to rethink their essential beauty regimen as they went back to work. While the tone of the event was lower key than many earlier livestreaming events, in keeping with the many challenges endured throughout the pandemic, viewers were treated to flash sales, virtual try-ons, and other opportunities to engage with the participating L'Oréal brands.

Livestreaming events such as "Back to Beauty" combine the excitement of a live sale with the interactivity of instant messaging as individual viewers' messages and likes are projected on the screen. Meanwhile, hosts try on products and deliver reviews on the spot during the livestream. Vouchers pop up on the screen and create a sense of urgency and entertainment. The event is promoted live on different social media platforms and generates engagement throughout the brands' platforms. Through its LazLive app, Lazada, the largest e-commerce platform in the region, also offers live karaoke sessions where online viewers can sing a duet with their favorite host. "Back to Beauty" was Lazada's first-ever cross-brand event featuring several

L'Oréal brands, including Garnier, L'Oréal Paris, and Maybelline, and a cross-category product selection, including makeup, skin care, and hair care.

The ability to organize and host such an ambitious and targeted event on a tight timeline is a testament to the strength of the L'Oréal-Lazada partnership. Throughout the world and across brands and divisions, L'Oréal has developed and nurtured strong ecosystems that bring together a wide range of upstream and downstream partners, from suppliers of ingredients to logistics providers, publishers, distributors, retailers, pure e-commerce players, hair stylists, influencers, beauty advisors, and the consumers themselves. The development of these ecosystems is one of the most critical elements of L'Oréal's all-encompassing, inside-out digital transformation.

From a Chain to an Ecosystem

"Business ecosystem" is a term that has become widely used by economics and business researchers as well as by managers in the past several decades and particularly in the digital era.[1] It is used somewhat ambiguously to refer both to the system of organic interactions that evolve between different parties who know they can benefit from building a relationship with each other, and to the strategically advantageous system that results from one company's efforts to develop these relationships. The intricate structure of most ecosystems reflects the increasing complexity companies face in offering innovative, highly relevant products and services to their customers in an environment where value can be either created or destroyed by any given ecosystem partner. Whereas value creation once followed a linear (value) chain consisting primarily of the unidirectional transfers of goods, information, and money, these simple chains have been drastically disrupted by the availability and transparency of information, enabling partners to benefit mutually from richer, multilateral, and often interdependent relationships where the traditional roles of supplier and customer lose much of their meaning. While the term "value chain" is still used, it fails to capture the complexity, nonlinearity, and interdependence of these multilateral relationships.

Take, for example, the multifaceted relationship between L'Oréal and Amazon—each of the two players is the other's customer, each providing unique value to the other's customers and sharing valuable content, data, knowledge, and other resources. As interactions become more complex and the specific roles of alliance partners less clear cut, the overall set of relationships built around a company or brand becomes more akin to an ecosystem than to a traditional value chain.

The ecosystem metaphor goes beyond the linguistic turn of phrase and captures the properties exhibited by these systems. These properties—which are common to a diverse range of complex systems such as living organisms, climate systems, cities, and more—make business ecosystems particularly powerful and effective in uncertain, fast-changing, and highly digitized environments such as the ones that L'Oréal and other large multinational companies are evolving. Ecosystems consist of "loosely interconnected participants who depend on each other for their mutual effectiveness and survival."[2] This makes ecosystem participants interdependent and pushes them toward collaboration, although they may also compete in certain domains that do not affect their interdependence. They are able to adapt efficiently to changes in their environment by combining and recombining resources and capabilities across different participants' boundaries.

In the case of business ecosystems, companies can tap into each other's capabilities as needed to deploy new solutions, allowing them to extend their competitive advantage efficiently, as in the example of L'Oréal's post-COVID livestreaming event on Lazada. The e-commerce and social commerce platform, a subsidiary of China's Alibaba, contributed its extensive knowledge of the Southeast Asian market and the ability to quickly set up a platform and promote it, together with the background logistics to enable the sales event. L'Oréal brought to the table the value of its brands, the demand for its products, its loyal customers, its own understanding of the consumer market, and its own online communications capabilities.

In this chapter, we will explore the reshaping of L'Oréal's value chain into a highly effective ecosystem or set of ecosystems as an important element of the company's digital transformation. Smaller ecosystems develop in specific markets, for specific brands or products, and are embedded into larger ecosystems. For instance, the ecosystem built around L'Oréal's Chinese e-commerce business is part of its larger China ecosystem, and also part of the company's global e-commerce ecosystem. Eventually, the smaller systems build up the broader global ecosystem, which encompasses all of L'Oréal's businesses worldwide together with its partners.

Shaping innovative alliances is hardly a new strategy for L'Oréal. In the late 1950s, L'Oréal played an important role in the development of the mass retail sector in France. Having spent significant time exploring the U.S. retail sector, then CEO François Dalle knew that supermarket chains were about to become the predominant retail channel for consumer goods and would yield tremendous control over manufacturers as they consolidated under a handful of large firms. The previous retail environment had been made up of local family-owned general and grocery stores with some consolidation under national brands. Manufacturers such as L'Oréal risked losing control of the positioning strategies they had carried out over decades, particularly in terms of pricing and in-store product placement. While self-service supermarkets seemed like a promising opportunity for L'Oréal's brands to attract more customers, the discounting policies of the increasingly powerful retailers jeopardized these brands' premium positioning.

Dalle was a founding member of an alliance of consumer goods manufacturers that helped design the rules of the game, guaranteeing ongoing bargaining power for manufacturers. Today, his achievements in this area have become part of the company's mythology, contributing to the image of L'Oréal as a powerful actor of modernization of the French retail sector.

Ecosystems' Key Attributes

Whereas the 1950s alliances had everything to do with gaining control and stability, the current context demands that ecosystems give up control and stability in favor of collaboration, complexity, speed, and flexibility. Companies looking to develop ecosystems must develop some of their key attributes: shared purpose among ecosystem players; focus on consumer solutions; structures and processes that enable the sharing of capabilities, including data; the ability to scale up fast; flexibility; and resilience.

Shared Purpose

When the first signs of the COVID-19 epidemic began to emerge in China, L'Oréal went into crisis mode, along with many of its Chinese suppliers. It quickly became obvious that the consumer demand that could no longer be fulfilled in brick-and-mortar stores had largely transferred to e-commerce channels. At the same time, L'Oréal managers saw a shift away from certain product categories, such as makeup, toward others, including skin care and wellness products. The production, logistical, and distribution implications were immense, and it became clear that the unprecedented crisis would test the agility of all of L'Oréal's operational teams as well as those of their partners.

Yanyan Zhang, L'Oréal China Supply Chain Director, identified as a key success factor the need for operational teams to increase their sensitivity and responsiveness to business needs driven by customer expectations. For this to happen, easy and speedy communication was critical. L'Oréal managers set up alternative communication channels with their partners to ensure continuity during the crisis using tools such as WeChat messaging. Supply chain teams were determined to deliver products to customers, in any possible way, no matter the channel.

To serve customers who opted to continue purchasing products in-store, IT teams developed in less than three weeks a WeChat-based app that enables beauty advisers to place orders and ensure delivery at the store counter. Finding solutions to the many operational issues demanded that L'Oréal and its suppliers and logistical partners share a real belief in one another's ability to problem-solve quickly, creatively, and decisively. Beyond the ability to communicate in real time, this feature of collaboration, called shared purpose,[3] consists of a highly focused common goal and the belief that there is no way to reach this desirable goal other than by working together. Zhang puts it this way: "When we are all together mentally, when we are all together spiritually, we can do a lot of things which seem impossible."

Challenges that demand instant decisions often require a preexisting level of trust if diverse players are even to engage in an often taxing problem-solving process, let alone commit to action. For L'Oréal China, partnerships were tested by the COVID-19 crisis in a way they had never been tested before. Many of these partnerships benefited from having been built on a robust shared purpose dynamic that was successfully pushed into higher gear at the onset of the crisis. Shared purpose lies at the core of the structure of ecosystems: not only does it require that collaborative partners share the same goal, it also rests on each partner's belief that they can only fulfill their goal in collaboration with the other(s). It is the focused goal and belief that make shared purpose–based collaborative partnerships perform so well in highly volatile and uncertain contexts.

Solution-Focused Collaboration

While L'Oréal China and its partners were able to step up their collaborative work at the onset of the COVID-19 crisis, developing team-based solutions is hardly new for the China unit. In its quest to penetrate the Chinese market by targeting different segments of the population with relevant offers, L'Oréal China identified an important job-to-be-done for adolescents: controlling their acne.

Acne is common among adolescents around the world, but Chinese youngsters have less access to professional skin-care advice, as China has only one dermatologist for every 60,000 inhabitants, roughly a third less than in the United States, and with much more uneven distribution. L'Oréal set out to find a solution to provide dermatologically sound diagnoses and treatment to Chinese youth, joining with two of its ecosystem partners: its network of dermatologists and its e-commerce partner, Alibaba. The Active Cosmetics Division, whose clinical brands include La Roche-Posay, Vichy, and SkinCeuticals, has a robust network of 160,000 dermatologists worldwide. Upstream, these partners contribute to the design and testing of products and services. Downstream, physicians act as prescribers and influencers.

The La Roche-Posay brand uses mineral-rich water from its own spring in western France to treat a range of serious skin ailments such as psoriasis, eczema, and damage resulting from harsh cancer therapies, as well as less serious issues, including acne. Alibaba's Tmall and Taobao, online shopping outlets, contributed artificial intelligence capabilities to the problem-solving partnership by aggregating and analyzing large quantities of data from user selfies. Using a neural network model based on deep learning, teams of developers and analysts collaborated in designing technology that correlates information taken from users' selfies with diagnostic profiles of skin conditions to identify the type of acne they suffer from.

As a result of the three-way partnership between the brand, the dermatologist network, and Alibaba, L'Oréal launched the Effaclar Spotscan app in 2019, providing Chinese acne sufferers with instant evaluation of their condition. Once diagnosed, users receive a recommended La Roche-Posay treatment or, in severe cases, are referred to participating dermatologists. As L'Oréal continues to develop nontraditional and multilateral partnerships, it is expanding the scope of its product portfolio and progressively building up its own tech capabilities. At the same time, its ecosystem partners benefit from the strong legitimacy associated with L'Oréal brands and their clinical partners, the company's deep knowledge of the skin care industry, its promotional resources, and the inherent value of the services offered to users of the platforms.

Capabilities Access

Few marketing functions have been as disrupted by digital transformation as media planning, the careful process of turning marketing strategy into executable plans and ad placement. As the availability, relevance, and usability of consumer data have multiplied, marketers have used these data to target consumers more precisely. Media buying, once considered an art requiring intuition and creativity, has turned into an algorithm-based exact science. By making the process more objective and giving marketers greater control over the way they manage their customers' journeys, the transformation has profoundly upended the relationship between marketers and their media agencies.

Whereas agencies once possessed the only key to effective targeting, the information and skills necessary are now readily available to advertisers as well. As the third-largest advertiser worldwide, L'Oréal has experienced the full force of this transformation and, in recent years, has taken steps to drastically rethink its marketing function. An important realization for brands was that the transformation must start from within and requires not just new skills but new mindsets and a new way of working both internally and with their agencies.

While some companies have chosen to bring the media-buying function in-house, in effect creating their own internal agencies, there are some drawbacks to this approach. Start-up costs are high, and companies struggle to attract the right talent and to maintain cutting-edge expertise and technology. For this reason, many large marketing companies, L'Oréal included, are opting for a hybrid option that combines the control they gain from the in-house option with the efficiency of outsourcing.

In 2019 L'Oréal UK and Ireland conducted a review of their media agency and selected a new agency, Essence, part of the WPP Group. Together, the UK unit and their new agency co-designed a collaborative structure they named Beauty Tech Labs. The creation of the hybrid client/agency unit reflects the belief within L'Oréal that ongoing trans-formation cannot be outsourced—it must come from within. By co-embedding the unit within L'Oréal and the agency, the client/agency team are looking to create a fully collaborative unit that learns and adapts together to evolving consumer needs, market opportunities, and technology. Staff from the two entities can play an important role in challenging each other to go beyond their current thinking and knowledge. Stéphane Bérubé, L'Oréal CMO for Western Europe, says bringing the external resources in-house makes L'Oréal a "much smarter client . . . elevating our knowledge and our expertise, (bringing) the discussion to another level."[4] On the agency side, getting to know L'Oréal's inner workings and, more importantly, their customers and offerings as intimately as if they were their own is an opportunity for agency staff to gain a much-needed and often-missing client-side per-spective and mindset.

The Beauty Tech Labs are set up as agile teams that can con-figure and reconfigure themselves to tackle projects and challenges as needed. Gayle Noah, the L'Oréal UK and Ireland media director who co-managed the review and decision with Bérubé, commented: "The whole thing is underpinned by a learning agenda—constantly moving forward, thinking about innovation, sprinting our key topics."[5] The innovative model is reflected in the remuneration solution put in place between the two partners, with key performance indicators (KPIs) built around an agreed-upon scope of work and outcomes, enabling the agency to garner the resources necessary to gear up for quality rather than volume.

Interdependence

No partnership serves as a better illustration of the interdependence between tech players and brands than the one forged by L'Oréal and Amazon. The relationship between the two giants has shifted over time as technology and markets have evolved, creating new opportu-nities for collaboration. Amazon sells L'Oréal products directly (as a so-called first party) through its own retail platforms, but it also carries L'Oréal-controlled shops on its third-party marketplace. For L'Oréal, Amazon functions as both a retailer and a competitor; it is a retail platform, a search engine, a media company, a data provider, and a fulfillment center.

As a media channel, Amazon publishes L'Oréal content, including tutorial videos, and serves as a review platform for consumers of L'Oréal brands. As Amazon customers review L'Oréal products, post tutorials, or share links with friends, they participate in L'Oréal's value-creating ecosystem, where they create or destroy value, as well as in Amazon's own ecosystem. For Amazon, L'Oréal brands are must-have pieces of the platform's beauty offer.

Another aspect of the interdependent relationship between the beauty giant and the e-commerce giant is L'Oréal's sale of its Modi-Face augmented-reality technology solutions to power Amazon's virtual makeup try-on app. The virtual try-on app is available across brands, serving L'Oréal's products as well as other manufacturers. Beyond goods and money, the two companies depend on each other to exchange knowledge and data that allow them to offer consumer solutions that amplify what each could achieve individually, creating synergistic value in a way that is simply not accounted for in a traditional value chain configuration. Because Amazon also competes with L'Oréal by marketing its own brand of products, the relationship between the two giants can best be described as "it's complicated" and illustrates the interdependence that develops among partners within an ecosystem.

Like many of its big-brand beauty competitors, L'Oréal resisted the lure of Amazon for years before finally agreeing to sell on Amazon's e-commerce platforms. Third-party vendors had been selling L'Oréal products in a quasi-gray market, without approval or control from the brands themselves. L'Oréal's more recent status as an official supplier and vendor has enabled sales of L'Oréal products on Amazon to surge, and the brands positioned themselves very well. Maybelline New York is Amazon's top beauty brand in the United States, with L'Oréal Paris in second position.

The shift in L'Oréal's policy toward Amazon was challenging, echoing the anguish felt in the 1950s within the company as supermarkets began selling some of L'Oréal's mass brands. Eventually, market reality was clear. CEO Jean-Paul Agon put it this way: "In e-commerce, the rule is always to cast your net where there are lots of fish. You're always going to find more customers searching on a generalist multibrand e-commerce site than on a brand's own site. Our sites are good at engaging with customers, at being where they want us to be, but we're not looking to compete with retailers."[6]

Ecosystems Perform in Times of Crisis ▬▬

Much of the power of ecosystems is their ability to perform in uncertain and volatile environments. They combine the strength and breadth of resource common to multiplayer partnerships with the versatility and nimbleness of ad hoc alliances, making them particularly good at delivering fast scaling and resilience in times of crisis.

Fast Scaling

While L'Oréal e-commerce sales had been growing at a steady pace, driven by a clear strategy to achieve a "reach" target of 50 percent of the company's business coming from e-commerce by 2030, the early months of 2020 saw a dramatic and unprecedented scaling of the company's e-commerce operations over a matter of days that completely redefined expectations for future growth capabilities. The company's ability to meet this drastic demand shift across divisions, functions, and countries left L'Oréal teams and leadership impressed and proud, and was met with strong approval by industry observers and analysts.[7] CDO Lubomira Rochet applauded the performance, noting how so much had been achieved in so little time.[8]

Even more remarkable is the fact that the acceleration appears to be long-lasting, suggesting that, far from a bubble effect, the e-commerce expansion represents a true scale-up of demand and performance, making the objective of 50 percent of sales online by 2030 seem eminently reachable. A similar effect was achieved on the advertising side with an acceleration of online spending from 50 percent to 70 percent of overall marketing budgets over the course of the lockdown period in the first quarter of 2020. L'Oréal's digital readiness has allowed an impressively fast scaling of digital capabilities to meet e-commerce demand and the need for a much greater digital proportion of media spend.

These successful results are testimony to the company's state of digital readiness in early 2020 as China went into lockdown, followed within weeks by much of the rest of the world. A profound dimension of this outcome is the breadth of capabilities that were harnessed in order to perform at the required level. Internal and external capabilities and resources ranging from supply chain management to production, logistics, distribution, marketing, and customer service were all deployed in a concerted and effective manner to enable the scaling of e-commerce, constituting another mark of a highly functional ecosystem. L'Oréal's e-commerce ecosystem is diverse and fast evolving. Pure players such as Amazon, Tmall, and Tmall's southeast Asian unit Lazada account for a large part of sales. E-retailers, the online arm of traditional retailers such as Hong Kong–based A.S. Watson or giant cosmetics retailers Sephora and Ulta also drive a significant share of the business. Other external channels include marketplaces such as the Japanese site Rakuten and Amazon's Marketplace.

While limited to a subset of L'Oréal brands, including NYX, Kiehl's, and Lancôme, and to certain countries, direct-to-consumer sales account for a growing part of the business. Players offering innovative e-commerce formats such as social commerce, livestreaming, and conversational commerce all saw significant sales hikes during the pandemic, establishing themselves quickly as strong ecosystem participants. L'Oréal has drawn valuable competitive advantage from its ability to roll out ModiFace, its virtual try-on engine, across many of the diverse e-commerce platforms, garnering it a desirable presence and visibility on many of these platforms. Virtual try-on, once a nice-to-have feature that enabled playful engagement with users, has become a must-have tool for online sales of makeup and cosmetics.

Livestreaming is one channel that illustrates the astounding scaling and inventiveness of L'Oréal's increasingly effective, digitally enabled ecosystem. Early incarnations of livestreaming arrived in the form of the several television home shopping networks that sprang up on cable television in the 1980s, primarily in North America. The leading home shopping network was U.S.-based QVC, started in 1986. QVC and its competitors carried product demonstrations hosted by B-list celebrities who encouraged viewers to call an oft-repeated toll-free number to buy the promoted products. The format continued to evolve over the years and was eventually picked up by Chinese platform Tmall and its livestreaming platform Taobao as an innovative and powerful tool for engaging with consumers.

Livestreaming, which has been referred to as "QVC on steroids," is behind the huge success of Tmall's Singles' Day, and accounts for a sizable portion of the strong performance of many Western beauty and fashion brands in the Chinese market over the past decade. The COVID-19 crisis has seen a doubling of livestreaming sales and a 700 percent increase in participating vendors in the Chinese market, helping to propel the innovative commerce format beyond China in an impressive manner. It is thanks to its strong ecosystem partnerships with a diverse range of players such as Tmall, Lazada, shopping platform Livescale, influencers, logistics providers, consumer communities, and more that L'Oréal has been able to scale its livestreaming activities, among other e-commerce efforts, so dramatically.

Tapping into the power of consumer communities was key to the success of livestreaming events built around 2020 Pride Week in the United States and Canada. Take the example of Urban Decay's Pride livestream makeup tutorial with Canadian drag queen Sofonda Cox, or NYX Cosmetics Pride Week makeup tutorial livestream with self-described "NYC Proud Fairy," 398-million-strong influencer Matt Bernstein (@MattXIV). What started as an opportunistic test to engage with shoppers during lockdown was quickly scaled up to a significant channel for L'Oréal beyond China. This could simply not have been achieved without the power and diversity of the strong ecosystem partnerships that L'Oréal has crafted and nurtured throughout its digital transformation, a worthy reincarnation of its legacy of robust relationships with suppliers and distributors.

Resilience

The severity of the COVID-19 crisis and its economic and social impacts have dramatically tested the resilience of L'Oréal as a company, along with its executives, its teams, and its ecosystems around the world. Many of the lessons learned within L'Oréal's Chinese ecosystem at the onset of the COVID-19 crisis informed decisions made throughout L'Oréal's global ecosystem as the pandemic spread throughout the world. The company expanded the problem-solving and decision-making practices it developed in China to the United States as well as to Europe, using locally adapted communication technology. And it offered financial support to vulnerable partners worldwide to help them survive the crisis. This support included measures such as financing raw material purchases for impacted suppliers as well as accelerating payments and extending credit terms for distributors, including hair salons, whose businesses had been shut down.

Some suppliers were enlisted to contribute to the production of hand sanitizer, which L'Oréal plants produced in several markets in response to the worldwide demand from first responders and medical professionals. Procurement experts from L'Oréal China supported the French government with the purchase from Chinese suppliers of personal protective equipment for French medical institutions. All these initiatives illustrate the resilience of L'Oréal's diverse ecosystems throughout the world.

Researchers have noted the similarities between the features of resilient biological ecosystems and business ecosystems. Several of these features—modularity, adaptation, redundancy, and heterogeneity—were successfully tested at L'Oréal in the COVID-19 crisis. Modular systems are built in such a way that individual constituents can act as circuit breakers to help prevent the collapse of the entire system under challenging conditions. In the early phase of the COVID-19 crisis, before the global spread of the epidemic, L'Oréal China and its local ecosystem performed in a modular way by containing the impact of the crisis within China, without severely affecting the rest of the global system.

Redundancies in the global ecosystem also contributed to resilience: in-store business swiftly shifted to e-commerce, and sharp declines in some product categories were quickly offset by dramatic increases in others. Across these major shifts, the global ecosystem proved its robust capacity for adaptation through experimentation, selection, and amplification of solutions from one part of the system to the others. Heterogeneity is another mark of resilience in ecosystems; the ability for heterogeneous components to respond in different ways mitigates the risk of global system failure. Heterogeneity is built into L'Oréal's decentralized structure. By allowing each local business unit and its system to find its unique solutions to the crisis, L'Oréal's broad ecosystem benefits from its heterogeneous nature and enhances its overall resilience.

******

The lessons learned from the COVID-19 crisis and L'Oréal's ability to activate its entire ecosystem during the crisis are particularly relevant in the context of a broader analysis of L'Oréal's digital transformation. Had the company not achieved a significant level of digital readiness before the unanticipated crisis, it would not have weathered the storm as well as it did.

Within the range of readiness dimensions are L'Oréal's powerful ecosystems of diverse players. A more traditional, less digitally enabled linear configuration of partnerships would not have performed as well. The performance of the broad ecosystem under conditions of huge stress confirms the importance of the human-based attributes of ecosystems, their shared purpose, their interdependence, and their solution-focused collaboration and capabilities sharing. Far from having moved away from deeply human and social relationships, digital transformation has enhanced the need for greater depth in these relationships. The message came through loud and clear from across the company: what made L'Oréal survive the crisis was the relationships within internal teams and with their external partners. China Supply Chain Director Yanyan Zhang's message of mental and spiritual togetherness, cited earlier, captured the true spirit of ecosystem collaboration. The extent of the transformation that has been achieved in this domain cannot be over-estimated. At the core of the ecosystem strategy, and implicit in Zhang's message, is the increased blurring of the lines between the company itself and its broader ecosystem. For a century-old legacy company like L'Oréal, in spite of its long history of openness to the outside world and support to its partners, the ecosystem logic requires a profound change in processes and culture.

TRANSFORMATION TIPS

- Turn your supply chain into an ecosystem that allows you to respond efficiently to unexpected circumstances by shifting resources and sharing knowledge.
- Just like customer centricity, ecosystems demand a drastic cultural shift throughout the organization.
- Ecosystem partnerships, just like customer centricity, demand greater openness and willingness to share but deliver greater value.
- Developing shared purpose within an ecosystem is key to its success.
- Interdependence is what holds an ecosystem together. No partner can succeed without the others.
- Resilience is an important attribute and benefit of ecosystems.
- The human element of ecosystems is a rich source of knowledge and provides support in a difficult and uncertain environment.

PUTTING PEOPLE FIRST

Stepping into Flexlab, L'Oréal's new research laboratory in Chevilly-Larue, just outside Paris, is like no lab experience you've ever had before. It is a truly people-centric facility, designed with the input of ninety staff members who volunteered over a period of four years to share insights, experiences, ideas, and desires, with the lab's designers and architects, and to test the facilities and equipment as they were developed. The lab experience is so disruptive that even the teams who participated in the lab's design were taken by surprise the first time they got to use it. The entire facility is easily reconfigured in under an hour by a team, without having to call facilities or IT support, in order to gear up for a project and foster creative thinking. All of the 140 workstations are on wheels and fully mobile, and most of the equipment is adjustable and multipurpose. The lab also sports state-of-the-art sustainability features. Focusing on the development of fragrances, skin care, and body care, the new lab is part of a network of eight research and innovation centers throughout France and twenty-one around the world.

The lab is linked by videoconferencing to other L'Oréal research locations around the world so teams across regions can be immersed in the same project and work together in real time, creating the practical basis for a connected innovation ecosystem. The lab design brief was to create an environment that would allow research teams to work more cross-functionally and collaboratively in support of the company's digital transformation; in other words, the design seeks to translate the principle of embedding digital at the heart of business into an organizational, cultural, and physical reality. Another aspect of this collaborative effort is the integration of open innovation into the research agenda, enabling joint innovation efforts with universities, start-ups, and suppliers and contributing to blurred lines between the company itself and its ecosystem. In this final chapter, we will dive deeply into the organizational and cultural aspects of the transformation and focus on the new ways of working that support the company's digital transformation, making it more digitally fit. Here again, we will explore how L'Oréal achieved its successful digital transformation by putting people first, in this case employees, in an effort sustained by the culture's deep roots and ability to evolve toward greater fitness.

We will highlight the eight features of what Jean-Paul Agon has called the most ambitious of the transformations he has spearheaded during his time as CEO at L'Oréal, the development and implementation of the Simplicity program, outlined in a "manifesto" and launched in 2016. The program was introduced as the result of long-running internal discussions within the executive committee about the fit between the company's culture and the outcomes of the extraordinary digital transformation that was taking place. The committee identified the need for a culture that is more responsive to the needs and expectations of its large global and diverse workforce and to the fast-changing competitive context in which it must perform as a digital organization. In other words, L'Oréal needed to make itself more attractive to new recruits and more supportive of its current employees while boosting its fitness and readiness for competition.

Prompting the executive committee discussion and the work that ensued was the realization that years of growth and expansion into new markets had resulted in increased levels of hierarchy and structural complexity, shifting the company away from its earlier relatively flat and light structure and making it less digitally fit. What was called for was a simpler organizational structure and a culture that promotes greater empowerment and collaboration. The Simplicity program was developed with the help of outside consultants in organizational sociology and internal taskforces who reported directly to Agon and the executive committee.

Simplicity is organized around four areas of focus: framing, feedback, cooperation, and meetings. Framing is about clearly setting the scope and parameters of any project, responsibility, or task. The focus on feedback aims to encourage transparent and honest dialog around performance, both in formal annual reviews and in casual daily interactions to foster greater trust and accountability. Cooperation is given renewed emphasis in order to shift away from individualistic behavior and toward performance. Finally, the manifesto calls for particular attention to meetings as the locus of efficient problem-solving and decision-making in the organization.

Beyond the four areas of focus, Simplicity defines eight "ways of working," or practices. Each of the practices is defined in relation to a previously entrenched behavior in order to clearly emphasize the expected behavioral shift. For instance, "cooperation is the new confrontation" encourages managers to move away from the previously accepted confrontational style toward cooperation and collective responsibility. The inherent paradox in the formulation of the older and newer practices means that they continue to be consistent with the deeper cultural pillars we detailed in Part I. The formulation of the eight practices, detailed in the sections below, picks up on L'Oréal's penchant for catchy phrases that are easily recalled and shared. Each of the sayings is rich in imagery and uses the trendy vernacular "X is the new Y," as encapsulated by the title of the comedy-drama web series *Orange Is the New Black*:

Teams Are the New Heroes

Customer Satisfaction Is the New Product Performance

Eat What You Cook Is the New Leave Before It Burns

Frame and Trust Is the New Control

Problem-Solving Together Is the New Meeting Behavior

Empowerment Is the New Management

Test and Learn Is the New Perfection

Cooperation Is the New Confrontation

Simplicity was rolled out across the L'Oréal organization in several ways. A general manifesto was distributed to employees around the world, setting out the four areas of focus and the eight ways of working. In each market and across divisions, teams worked in a bottom-up manner to interpret the new practices in a way that was relevant to their culture and to integrate it into their own context. This helped employees familiarize themselves with the program and fashion it to better meet local expectations and constraints. This methodology echoes the initial light-touch diffusion of the digital transformation process, in which each country developed its own initiatives in a decentralized, grass-roots manner in response to a clear and decisive impulse from the top.

Simultaneously and throughout the company, managers were asked to join a large-scale management transformation course called Lead & Enable for Simplicity. Based on behavior change methodologies, the program aims to increase individual flexibility and enhance strategic vision while providing tools to facilitate team collaboration and co-creation. More than 10,000 employees worldwide were trained in the first two years of the program.

While the Simplicity program was led separately from the digital transformation, it is hard to dissociate the two efforts. Simplicity was largely prompted by the need to make the organization better equipped for the digital world, and in turn the program has clearly enabled L'Oréal to sustain and accelerate the digital transformation process. As we review and illustrate each of the eight practices, we'll show how it integrates into the broader cultural transformation and supports the company's digital fitness. We have touched upon the eight practices throughout the previous chapters, but it is their role within the broader transformation of L'Oréal that we are most interested in emphasizing here. As a whole, the Simplicity program constitutes the human side of this broad transformation and confirms that the success of L'Oréal's transformation has been about putting people first.

Teams Are the New Heroes

The cult of the hero has always been an important aspect of L'Oréal's culture. Eugène Schueller's story and legacy are well known to all L'Oréalians. The three subsequent CEOs (excluding Charles Zviak, who remained at the helm less than three years because of ill health), François Dalle, Lindsay Owen-Jones, and Agon, have each been celebrated as larger-than-life characters for their individual achievements and their lasting legacy. The traditional cradle-to-grave career path encouraged the myth of the hero. Individual managers, Frenchmen for the most part, climbed to senior positions by piling up remarkable feats in far-flung countries, later returning to headquarters with titillating stories of markets conquered and competitors crushed. While the achievements were unquestionably impressive, much was left out of these accounts. None of these splendid careers would have been possible without a culture and a system that privileged young male executives from top French business schools (ours included) and gave those who showed the right motivation, intellect, and temperament huge opportunities to learn and succeed. Hard work and ambitious results were expected, but the rewards—financial, social, and professional—were proportionately attractive.

The resulting culture of the hero entertained a strong individualistic tendency that, for many of the promising young managers, dated back to their days in their pre–business school *classes préparatoires*, the uniquely French and social class–preserving system of private undergraduate institutions that leads to the quota-based business school admissions competitions. In these schools, self-centered behavior was the norm, and was neither frowned upon nor challenged.

Much has changed to disfavor this type of behavior at L'Oréal and in other large organizations. As L'Oréal achieved greater success in international markets, cohorts of local managers acceded to higher echelons, bringing cultural diversity to the makeup of executive teams. At the same time, more women entered the senior management and executive ranks, bringing with them different styles of behavior and expectations while vying for the same opportunities as their male counterparts. As external competition intensified and accelerated, successful performance came from teams that worked well together rather than from individuals who competed with one another. As the company entered the digital era, diversity and collaboration went from nice-to-have attributes to must-have imperatives.

Human resource policies and practices caught up with these changes and institutionalized collective rather than individual performance. The formulation of the "teams are the new heroes" practice is part of this institutionalization process: it leaves room for heroic behavior and for the myth of the hero as an element of storytelling and mythmaking, but moves the focus from the individual to the collective.

The COVID-19 crisis has prompted many heroic team performances, among them the work of logistical teams worldwide that adapted their operational and transportation strategies overnight to accommodate the sudden shifts in demand and distribution, prompting CDO Rochet to refer to them as the true heroes of the crisis. The work of many of these teams has now been documented and celebrated in a series of short videos detailing their exploits, entitled "Beyond the Crisis: My Job Tomorrow." In one of the videos, Marc Antoine Poulle, Supply Chain Director for L'Oréal Travel Retail Asia Pacific, waxes lyrical as he recalls his team's remarkable ability to set up temporary distribution centers, activating alternative transport routes and mobilizing new suppliers overnight, all the while keeping their eye on strategic objectives such as sustainability goals. Asked what his core learning has been from the crisis, Poulle is quick to identify his team's capacity, agility, and resilience under extremely challenging circumstances. Commenting on the future, he points to his team's readiness to take on increasing challenges and burgeoning opportunities in a fast-changing environment by using data to better anticipate market shifts, and discusses bringing more automation into operations while continuing to deliver on sustainability objectives.

Customer Satisfaction Is the New Product Performance

The second of the Simplicity practices is a canonization of customer centricity and a recognition that, far from being a marketing precept, it must be ingrained as a cultural mindset and a business objective. Built into the customer satisfaction practice is also an implied picture of a more open organization that brings together the wide range of partners that can indeed deliver customer satisfaction, constituting a high-performing and diverse ecosystem. As we've seen in previous chapters, by putting customers first, the company is positioning itself at the core of an ecosystem that includes both internal and external partners, all working in unison to create value in the form of customer satisfaction.

The transition from product centricity to customer centricity is notoriously difficult for traditional companies, no matter their historical focus on customers. The transition requires a cultural and organizational shift, as well as the acquisition of specific capabilities. Not only do mindsets and practices need to change drastically and systems transform to account for new data collection, performance evaluations, and decision-making processes, but the organization must be restructured in such a way that customer journeys are properly managed from start to finish. Processes and systems need to be put in place to understand

and manage customer experience and to create innovative solutions that enhance customer satisfaction.

L'Oréal's acquisitions of Kiehl's, NYX, and Urban Decay, all three of which joined the group as highly effective customer-centric organizations, have helped move the needle on all three of these dimensions by sharing their best practices and changing mindsets. More recently, L'Oréal added Pulp Riot, a professional hair coloring company, to its portfolio of innovative customer-centric brands. This American brand has grown by creating cutting-edge content and using social media to inspire and educate hairstylists.

While L'Oréal's Professional Products Division was built on nurturing strong relationships with professionals, there was a clear need for greater digital capabilities to enhance these relationships. From stylist support to enabling virtual try-ons for customers and at-home tutorials, there is plenty of room for L'Oréal to add greater value to its relationship with salons and to the relationship between hair professionals and their clients using digital and tech tools.

Beyond developing customer centricity through acquisitions, L'Oréal has identified promising new customer-centric beauty tech solutions, thanks to its global open innovation team's work with start-ups. Recent ventures include a platform that sets up and manages sampling programs for beauty brands, a "nailbot" that designs and prints nail patterns, an influencer co-creation platform, and a social commerce community for beauty enthusiasts. Not only do these start-ups and the entrepreneurial ecosystem built around them develop promising customer solutions, they also serve to inject new ideas, processes, networks, and excitement within the entire organization.

Eat What You Cook Is the New Leave Before It Burns

Perhaps the most evocative of the practices, "Eat what you cook" promotes a long-term business approach. While patience and a long-term perspective were part of L'Oréal's early culture, as illustrated by the decade-long development of the Japanese market, recent years have seen a tendency to look for quicker wins, accelerate product cycles, and an attitude of "leave before it burns." Pressure from financial markets and the need to defend product differentiation have driven a tendency for many companies to focus on short-term performance objectives. In this context, eating what you cook, or giving your investments sufficient time to pay off, may seem paradoxical, but it is also eminently pragmatic. It is in fact a recognition that the company as a whole is still in learning mode when it comes to tech and digital expertise and can afford extra time to develop the right levels of competences.

While the businesses were eventually assessed a poor fit for L'Oréal's brand portfolio, both The Body Shop and Clarisonic were handled with patience and a long-term perspective rather than abandoned at the first sign of trouble, and they provided excellent opportunities for learning about retail and skin care devices, respectively. No one at L'Oréal could be accused of having failed to give either of the two subsidiaries a proper chance.

Two areas in which L'Oréal is adopting a deliberately long-term approach are sustainability and social responsibility. These two domains have been designated as strategic by Agon and given the same level of visibility and priority as the digital and cultural transformations they complement. Since 2013, the Sharing Beauty with All program has pulled together all the corporate initiatives around sustainable innovation, production, and consumption. The program really is about taking on the responsibility of eating what you cook, as it considers some of the serious threats to sustainability posed by digital technology.

E-commerce, for instance, constitutes an environmental challenge because of the toll associated with packaging and transportation. While solutions are being developed, they have not yet been sufficient to make e-commerce environmentally neutral. A long-term approach to e-commerce requires solutions and policies that will turn it into a sustainable consumption practice for decades to come. The same goes for the manufacturing of highly personalized products, which reduce production efficiency. In addition to mitigating the environmental effects of digitally enhanced production and distribution, eating what you cook is also about finding efficient digital solutions to sustainability issues. During the COVID-19 crisis, videoconferencing solutions were deployed throughout the company to enable real-time worldwide communications. As was the case in many other global companies, the efficiency and high performance of these solutions will undoubtedly continue to reduce the need for international travel and its high carbon impact.

Also under the broad umbrella of Sharing Beauty with All, the Share & Care program delivers a range of benefits aimed at the broader ecosystem, including employees, partners, and local communities. It guarantees a standard level of employee benefits and policies defined globally and adapted to regional and local standards. These benefits include health care coverage, parental leave, well-being support, and more.

As part of its long-term focus, Share & Care also includes social innovation labs set up across regions to develop new ways of delivering greater social impact within the company and throughout its ecosystem. Some of the initiatives that have come out of these labs include flexible working arrangements deployed across certain markets, including India, where 25 percent of the workforce has taken advantage of the opportunity. Other flexible opportunities include job sharing aimed at attracting more parents with child-care responsibilities into the workforce, and flex learning that allows employees to choose different professional development paths. A Brazilian program for families has increased maternity leave beyond the legal requirement and provides flu shots to employees and their families, as well as physical fitness assessments and coaching. Here again, these social impact programs are very much about eating what you cook.

Having greatly benefited from the many diverse markets in which it operates and from the work of its local employees, L'Oréal fulfills its social responsibility to provide these valuable employees an equitable level of benefits and to contribute to their communities. Agon refers to these initiatives as triggers of a virtuous cycle that drives motivation, well-being, and a sense of belonging, as well as a real drive to improve performance.[1] Putting people first is both the right thing to do and the smart way to run a transformative business.

Finding a common purpose between their personal and professional lives is an increasingly sought-after element of well-being for employees, particularly millennials. Many initiatives have been launched in recent years to enable employees to express their personal purpose through work. One such program is Citizen Day, which allows employees to devote some of their working hours to a local organization of their choice. The program has recently been expanded into Citizen Skills, an initiative that invites employees to expand their involvement with nonprofits throughout the year.

Beyond doing the right thing and motivating employees, these initiatives are good for the company. Many are offered across sites and open up opportunities for employees with different functions, skills, and levels of seniority to meet and share new ideas. Employees working on non-work-related projects are in effect given a chance to think outside of their regular professional constraints, a process that drives creativity, particularly team creativity. By opening up its ecosystems to the non-profit organizations for which employees volunteer, L'Oréal expands its global sphere of influence and its ability to innovate. Because many of these initiatives fulfill the needs and expectations of millennial employees, they also allow the company to compete more effectively with other employers, such as start-ups and tech companies, for the most qualified talent.

The issue of diversity and inclusion has been identified as strategic by Agon and the executive committee. But the focus of these initiatives has shifted in recent years away from communicating about these efforts to having a meaningful real-world impact. According to Deputy CEO, soon-to-be CEO Nicolas Hiéronimus, "When you make a statement about inclusion, it is expected that it should be authentic, that it should address the company's relationship to the world in a meaningful way."[2] As discussed in the previous chapter, this has meant casting the spotlight on empowering women, promoting gender equality, and supporting LGBTQ rights. The company has made significant strides in these domains and is keenly measuring the positive impact of these efforts on employee satisfaction and performance, as well as in external recognition and "employer brand" reputation.

One area of diversity and inclusion that has come under greater public scrutiny is cultural and ethnic diversity. L'Oréal's UK division has invited Munroe Bergdorf, the Black transgender influencer who had accused the company of unfair dismissal and paying lip service to the Black Lives Matter movement, to join a newly formed UK-based diversity committee. This incident illustrates the critical need for global companies—whose diverse employees, customers, partners, and other stakeholders they depend on for their success and performance—to constantly reexamine their commitments to diversity and inclusion. A "people first" digital transformation requires nothing less than continuous proactive action to implement measures that deliver on these commitments.

Frame and Trust Is the New Control

Frame is one of the four areas of focus of the Simplicity program. An important aspect of L'Oréal's culture, it serves as the basis for management as well as business decisions. Careful framing of problems, challenges, projects, or initiatives means that they are clearly defined and scoped out before an analysis is conducted and a solution sought and found.

Framing is the rigorous analytical basis of much of L'Oréal's more creative problem-solving and decision-making. Take, for instance, the work of Christophe Prud'homme, Global Purchasing Director for Makeup Packaging, and his teams during the COVID-19 crisis. Prud'homme and his team had to shift frames mid-crisis from operational firefighting to strategic risk management. The first phase required careful identification of available resources while the second was about analyzing scenarios for risk mitigation.

Framing is particularly critical when problem-solving is conducted in teams. Unless all team members understand and agree on the scope and constraints associated with a given project, inefficiency sets in. At the onset of the COVID-19 crisis, the challenge for Prud'homme and his team was to solve immediate issues such as identifying those partners whose factories were closing down and were unable to continue supplying packaging materials. This required that they work closely with suppliers, setting up instant messaging communication channels and troubleshooting in real time. Alignment was key to ensuring proper supply of the materials required to meet demand as it shifted both geographically and in terms of categories.

Later in the crisis, the frame shifted toward the midterm to long-term strategic challenge of supporting longstanding supply chain partners and analyzing and mitigating risk within the supply chain, again requiring alignment between teams of analysts working on forecasting, risk management, and strategy. Clearly defining these two different frames and shifting from one to the other helped maintain an agile and efficient approach under challenging conditions and focus the team's efforts.

Beyond these two frames, however, Prud'homme identifies the sustainability imperative as an overarching frame throughout the crisis. Defining frames is also key to the success of trust-based management systems. Once a frame has been defined, teams can be trusted to seek solutions within the frame, thus reducing the need for close supervision and the inefficiencies that come with it. The very notion of framing can seem paradoxical in a company such as L'Oréal, where creativity and innovation are prized. Working within a frame means thinking inside a box, just what new recruits are trained not to do. So, yes, frames are important and help define the scope of a project, but no, they are not carved in stone and they can be questioned. Any deviation from the frame must then be documented and argued.

Frame and trust are important elements of the feedback focus within Simplicity. Once a clear frame has been established, feedback is essential to enable trust to flourish. Honest dialogs about performance foster accountability and build trust.

Framing and trust are foundational to L'Oréal's decentralized model. As discussed in Chapter 1, in its first few years, before Lubomira Rochet came on board as CDO, digital transformation consisted of a multitude of individual initiatives carried out at the local level. The initial framing by Agon was broad and left plenty of room for local improvisation. In subsequent years, under Rochet's leadership, narrower frames were set around different projects such as precision marketing, e-commerce, data, and more. The frame and trust principle has served the digital transformation process well. Conversely, digital technology can often make it easier to communicate frames and to set and implement the kinds of checks and balances that foster trust.

Problem-Solving Together Is the New Meeting Behavior

One area of significant frustration in many organizations is the proliferation of endless meetings that do not produce any tangible results and fail to contribute to performance. Without needing to consult organizational experts, most frequent meeting attendees will confirm that the source of the problem is the failure to structure and manage meetings effectively, the frequent lack of a clear agenda, and the poor motivation of most meeting attendees. Simplicity addresses the issue by setting a clear purpose for every meeting—it must be about collective problem-solving.

This purpose is set within the broader frame of Simplicity's purpose, which is to make the organization better at solving the multitude of problems that come from operating in a complex and fast-changing environment. Meetings must be results focused, which means that they must be about collective problem-solving. Beyond simple agenda setting, making problem-solving the purpose of a meeting also helps determine other meeting elements such as who is invited, who chairs the meeting, how long the meeting will take, where it will be held, and how it will unfold. As part of the Lead & Enable program, managers receive training and coaching in these areas. Feedback is also part and parcel of the new meeting behavior. The Human Resources department introduced an app for meeting organizers to collect feedback from all meeting participants with five simple questions that assess the value of the meeting and each participant's contribution, as well as the effect of the meeting on each participant's motivation to continue working on the project at hand.

The increased availability of data has given managers the ability to evaluate the results of their actions in real time, and, as a result, furnished much greater clarity on what problems they need to solve. In a predigital, pre-data world, identifying poor performance on a given indicator such as customer retention in a certain market would happen with a significant time lag of one or two quarters. Pinpointing the root causes of the poor performance was often an inexact science, at best. Data makes performance issues stand out in a crystal-clear and inescapable way and can often point straightforwardly to their root causes. As a result, much of the work conducted in a digital organization is around problem-solving: we can see that our customer retention numbers are soft in a certain market and we know why. What are we going to do about it now?

The "problem-solving together" practice also emphasizes the collective aspect of problem-solving in meetings. Collective creative work, which problem-solving is, requires that participants interact with one another in real time in order for ideas to be put on the table (whether the table is real or virtual). Problem-solving starts with participants expressing and listening to one another's ideas. This back-and-forth process of translating ideas into words and words back into ideas is the powerful basis of collective creativity. Participants imagine and reimagine ideas and solutions based on their own interpretation of what is shared. Each individual's interpretation is based on the context in which they operate, on their knowledge of the situation, on their previous experience of similar situations, and more. For this reason, diversity of backgrounds and styles is an important element of success in collective problem-solving. As ideas are shared, they are debated, analyzed, and transformed along the way toward greater relevance. Little by little, solutions begin to emerge, gain consensus, and are retained. Leaders are trained in how to frame problems, ask questions, challenge premises, encourage contributions, guide conversations, and create consensus in order to optimize productive problem-solving and make meetings truly value enhancing.

Empowerment Is the New Management

Meet Shane Wolf, Global President of U.S. brands in the Professional Products Division. Wolf, a hair professional by training and a farmer by birth, had always wanted to bring these two important elements of his life together. Under the auspices of L'Oréal's internal incubator, Wolf founded Seed Phytonutrients, the first farm-to-beauty hair, face, and body brand that uses seed extracts in its formulas.

When Wolf traveled from Bucks County, Pennsylvania, to Paris to pitch his venture to L'Oréal's incubator team, he was determined to pull out all the stops. He filled suitcases with seeds and his own seed-based concoctions and even brought along recordings of his favorite bluegrass music to create the perfect atmosphere during the pitch. Whether it was his music, his well-rehearsed presentation, or the compelling business case he articulated, Wolf's pitch was successful, and Seed Phytonutrients was launched in 2018 as a new L'Oréal brand.

Wolf's story illustrates the start-up spirit that pervades L'Oréal. As part of Simplicity, this spirit of entrepreneurship has been nurtured and empowered and has replaced a more traditional and constraining management approach. At all levels of the organization, employees like Shane Wolf are encouraged to spread their wings and create and pitch initiatives small and large. While not all employee-led initiatives turn into new brands, many bring real value to the business, regardless of their scale.

This level of empowerment in an organization as large as L'Oréal is remarkable, and requires excellent judgment on the part of leaders. The right balance between empowerment and strict supervision is not so easy to find and demands clear framing, processes, and rules. Junior employees, including interns, are taught to think outside their job purview and imagine ways to add value to the business. They are trained to analyze opportunities, build a case to support their proposal, and pitch their ideas to more senior audiences. The process is reminiscent of one we described in Chapter 2, in which managers were invited to the "confrontation room" to be drilled on their ideas. The difference today is in the approach—gone is the confrontation, replaced with a rigorous but supportive and trusting attitude that helps junior staff develop the confidence they need to put their best foot forward. This kind of empowerment is a sure way to nurture the kind of creative and audacious thinking and work that are key to innovation.

Another aspect of empowerment is the flattening of the hierarchy and the informality it fosters. Junior employees and managers are given ample opportunities to work alongside more senior leaders and empowered to contribute to meetings and discussions. A fascinating illustration of this blurring of hierarchical barriers is the reverse mentoring program put in place in 2016 as a way to help older senior managers and executives become better acquainted with digital technology by learning about it from junior "digital natives." Older and younger individuals are paired up and work together. While not unique to L'Oréal, the scheme, which was originated by former GE CEO Jack Welch, epitomizes many of the overlapping aspects of L'Oréal's digital transformation and its Simplicity program. Tugcan Sebit, a young Turkish employee in the finance department, started as an intern and was paired with a senior executive. For him, reverse mentoring is a great development tool that helps build bridges between generations. It gave him a quick and efficient introduction to company culture and helped him feel like a valuable part of the organization from the very beginning. By having a chance to support a senior leader and to discuss strategic issues with him, Sebit quickly felt that he was able to develop creative ideas and present them to his managers.

Beyond gaining exposure to digital knowledge and expertise, senior managers who participate in reverse mentoring get a chance to better understand the mindset of younger employees and listen to their concerns. It also helps them gain insights into their management style and how it is perceived by younger employees. For both generations, reverse mentoring constitutes an excellent way to experience a true collaboration, where each participant has something to give and to gain.

Test and Learn Is the New Perfection

As we discussed in Chapter 3, the test and learn approach is an important aspect of digital transformation and also stands at the core of any successful learning organization that accepts the premise that there is no such thing as a state of perfect or definitive knowledge. As part of the Simplicity program, L'Oréal has made learning and upskilling a central part of its culture.

One of the key challenges early in the digital transformation process was to create a baseline of digital skills across all marketing functions at L'Oréal. The company partnered with General Assembly, a digital and tech training company, to develop a series of digital marketing skills tests for existing staff and job applicants. Based on test results, individuals were allocated to training programs for upskilling.

While a great deal of emphasis was placed on upskilling existing employees, some highly specialized positions were at first difficult to fill internally and required an extensive recruitment effort. These jobs included data scientists, media traders, search engine optimization experts, social media and community managers, e-commerce specialists, and more. In order to facilitate the integration of these new staff members, an onboarding app called Fit Culture was launched in 2017. Co-created by L'Oréal HR teams and their new recruits, Fit, as it is known, is available in eleven languages across thirty countries. It supports newcomers, helping them understand the company culture over the course of their first month at work, using employee testimonials as well as games, quizzes, and small projects.

Over recent years, as the overall organization has gained greater expertise in digital domains, and as digital has become the default approach in marketing and across functions, the distinction between recently recruited digital experts and upskilled employees has blurred. Fewer people retain a digital designation in their titles as digital becomes the norm, and many of the original digital experts have now also crossed into business positions.

The shift away from a culture of perfection to a culture of learning goes beyond building new skills; it is also a matter of accepting ongoing contextual and market change rather than stability. One of the most difficult aspects of digital transformation is the acceptance that ongoing change is unavoidable and permanent. As the pace of change has accelerated and L'Oréal has proven its ability to understand and withstand both drastic and ongoing change, and to adapt to it successfully, most remaining reluctance or resistance within the organization has vanished, and the culture has shifted successfully away from perfection toward learning.

Another crucial element in achieving full digital buy-in across the organization has been the wholesale and visible engagement of senior leaders. Early on, the CDO team developed a number of initiatives to turn the top rung of the organization into believers and advocates. In true digital manner, gamification was part of the learning process through its highly popular proprietary business game Wine Game, set in the wine industry, which was played by executives throughout the company. In addition, learning expeditions were organized for the company's thousand top executives to visit leading tech companies in Silicon Valley and the Pacific Northwest and meet with their own executives. These experiences enabled them to imagine and build their own digital roadmaps and begin advocating digital transformation within their organizations.

Cooperation Is the New Confrontation

One year after the conclusion of the 2018 FIFA World Cup in Moscow, another worldwide sporting event took place in June 2019, the fifteenth annual L'Oréal World Cup. For two days, twelve football teams and twelve volleyball teams competed against each other, bringing together three hundred employees from fourteen countries worldwide. Regardless of their position in the company, the players come together to share their commitment and passion, their respect for one another, and their shared purpose and perseverance. Beyond providing a fun and exciting opportunity for participants to compete with colleagues from around the world, the L'Oréal World Cup makes for a powerful illustration of the cooperative mindset that is a crucial precept of the Simplicity program. Team sports combine the two elements of cooperation and competition, a paradox that is also at the heart of L'Oréal's new cultural approach. In sports as in business organizations, healthy competition and the robust challenging of others' ideas are beneficial, but they must remain within an overall perspective of cooperation and teamwork.

For a number of reasons, a digitally transformed company operating under customer centricity cannot function without adopting collaboration. The first has to do with the need for cross-functionality. As companies focus on providing integrated solutions to customers at every point of their customer journeys, internal collaboration must be activated in order to deliver integration. Ensuring that a consumer who buys a Lancôme lipstick online can return it to a Lancôme store requires cross-functional collaboration between the e-commerce and retail teams on a common CRM system as well as a determination to problem solve together to serve their mutual customer. Teams with very different competences and mindsets are brought together and must learn to speak the same language: the e-commerce team with its strong digital focus and the retail team with its commercial approach.

Beyond cross-functionality, collaboration is also required to harness the breadth of knowledge in the organization and enable agility and innovation. Information technology teams are key participants in many digital transformation projects. L'Oréal brought its IT department into the early stages of the digital transformation process and trained IT teams to support the transformation using agile methodology. IT staff learned to collaborate with business teams by using basic agile user-centric principles such as putting end users at the heart of solutions and allowing solutions to evolve over time, measuring outcomes including user experience, and building in user validation at each development stage. Although this collaborative approach worked well, generating relevant solutions and shorter development times, IT teams were not equipped, in the early days of digital transformation, to sufficiently align with their operational colleagues' business objectives. This changed in 2018 when IT was moved from the administration and finance department to the operations division, opening the way for greater alignment, shared purpose, and collaboration.

It is by aligning on purpose and objectives, either across functions or across geographies, that the kind of knowledge sharing and problem-solving that is critical to uncertain and fast-changing contexts, such as those experienced during the COVID-19 crisis, can be triggered. Lessons learned from China early in the crisis were shared collaboratively with other countries and helped speed up these countries' ability to respond efficiently once the pandemic spread around the world. This is where L'Oréal reaps the greatest rewards of its simplified organization and culture, in being able to quickly redirect its energy, its knowledge, and its resources at any given point in time where the needs are the greatest, all the while accumulating expertise and information.

******

The secrets to L'Oréal's successful digital transformation are many. Among them, the wholesale organizational and cultural transformation that started with the Simplicity program in 2016 is possibly the best kept and the most potent. Changing the way people at L'Oréal work with one another, think of their collective success, trust one another, learn and play together, and share important values has not just helped support the organization's digital transformation, but turned it into a beneficial transformation for all its employees worldwide. By putting its own people first in conducting its transformation, L'Oréal has ensured that the success of the company has also benefited the people who make it up.

TRANSFORMATION TIPS

- A cultural transformation must be part of any digital transformation.
- Cultural and digital transformations can be managed separately but must be consistent and must complement each other.
- Grounding your digital transformation into your organization's cultural foundation helps create continuity and bring reassurance to the organization.
- A decentralized structure works well to enable grassroots buy-in and participation, and constitutes a powerful complement to a strong and consistent message from the top.
- Deliver key messages in a clear and compelling manner and integrate them into a broader learning and development strategy. Provide opportunities for units to experiment with the new norms and mindset.
- Put people first in all aspects of your digital transformation.

Conclusion

The story we have told is simple and age-old. As a community goes about its business, serving others through their craft and trade, a watchful leader gives the signal that trouble is on the way. The community leader understands that this incoming threat could be turned into an opportunity for a better life if only the community could seize the moment and transform itself swiftly enough. She stands up and speaks out to the community. Because she is well respected as a competent and fair leader, the community heeds her warning and begins to prepare for transformation.

People will need to take on new and different roles that will make them better able to manage the changes to come. The community rethinks how people communicate and asks: How can we get better connected and respond more quickly as the unexpected happens? How can we benefit from one another's experience and knowledge more efficiently? The community also reconsiders its relationships to the outside world. Wouldn't it be better if we could count on others outside our own walls to help us deal with the incoming changes? After all, outsiders depend on us as much as we depend on them. Wouldn't it be best if the outsiders felt just as involved in helping us survive as we do, and if we banded together? And what if all the people we've served over the years came together to tell us what matters most to them and help us grow stronger? We could serve them even better in the future.

As she tells this story to her people, the community leader is hopeful. She is fortunate, having inherited and grown a community that thrives on creative thinking, openness, curiosity, and pragmatism. Of course, she'll have to overcome resistance. Change is inherently uncomfortable for most humans. The threat isn't quite visible to the less careful observer and life in the community has been very comfortable in recent years. But the lessons of the past, from the early days when the settlers formed the community and gave it its key principles, have served to instill a sense of adventure and a willingness to try things out.

This is not a story about tech changes; it is a story about human adaptiveness, creativity, and the yearning for a more fulfilling way of working, of creating valuable experiences for ourselves and others.

In telling L'Oréal's digital transformation story, we have demystified what digital transformation is about and shown that at the heart of it all is simply a renewed attention to human needs, social interactions, collaboration, and diversity and inclusion—and to giving people a voice. Digital transformation doesn't have to be about putting tech and data first; it must be about adapting tech and data to humans.

As we finish the story, it is evident to us that what happened at L'Oréal is special in many ways, but also not so special. L'Oréal's transformation, far from picture perfect, has been led with conviction and deftness by a highly experienced and competent CEO and his equally experienced and competent senior team. But in many ways, the transformation that took place at L'Oréal is an encapsulation of the transformation most of us live through in our personal and professional lives. The disruption wave has also engulfed all of us in the way we work, the way we relate to one another, and the way we buy things, and has forced us to reinvent many aspects of our lives at home and at work. In our introductory chapter, we shared a personal example of the disruption in our teaching practices. We know that you, our reader, have lived through similar disruptions and transformed your own practices. The kinds of changes we have made in our teaching and that we've witnessed at L'Oréal, far from driving a more impersonal experience, can drive greater focus on core human elements. They leave more time for emotions and feelings, for the subtleties and warmth of human relationships, for the creative quirks that make all the difference in someone's day. Digital transformation can be used—we have seen it—as a way to bring the human back into commerce.

It is our sincere hope that this demystification will allay some of the natural anxieties and concerns many of us experience when it comes to leading or experiencing digital transformation. By setting the story in the context of the beauty industry, a deeply human-focused domain, we wanted to reinforce the people-first focus. Whether you read the book cover to cover or focused on the chapters that most spoke to your needs and took in our Transformation Tips, we urge you to be alert and to rally those around you in undertaking this kind of transformation. Tell them to fasten their seatbelts and come with you on an exciting ride that will enable them to do more and to do better. It can be a bumpy ride, as our friends at L'Oréal will tell you, but it is the ride of a lifetime, and it is certainly worth it.

Acknowledgments

This book was in the making for a little over two years. During that time, we benefited from support, inspiration, and input from many people whom we would like to acknowledge and thank from the bottom of our hearts.

Many people at L'Oréal contributed by generously providing us with rich and relevant information and, more specifically, with honest and insightful accounts of their own experience and opinions. These include Jean-Paul Agon, who supported our book project from the beginning and kindly agreed to write the Foreword, in addition to sitting down for an interview on a particularly busy week. We would like to sincerely thank three other members of the Executive Committee: Frédéric Rozé, Lubomira Rochet, and Stéphane Rinderknech, who also kindly took the time to answer our questions. Frédéric Rozé provided many insights on the U.S. market, and Stéphane Rinderknech on the China market. Lubomira Rochet was extremely generous in sharing her views on digital transformation and taking us through many aspects of the roadmap she designed and implemented at L'Oréal. She validated many of our hypotheses along the way and encouraged us repeatedly. Her support meant so much to us. Jean-Claude Le Grand, also a member of the Executive Committee, has provided ongoing support to both Marie and Béatrice.

Other key supporters at L'Oréal have been: Rémy Simon, whom we both thank for his huge support and help in coordinating interviews and some of the material that appears in the book. More personally, Béatrice would like to thank Rémy for his friendship, as well as all the people at L'Oréal who have aided her work on the company for more than twenty years. Guive Balooch has supported much of Marie Taillard's work, and she wishes to thank him. Marie also thanks Luka Brekalo, a former student, loyal supporter, and friend, who has opened up many doors and shared many ideas. Nicolas Pauthier provided excellent insights on the organizational aspects of the transformation, along with Arnaud Vautier. Matthieu Serres shared his experience of the Simplicity program and we wish to thank him. Other key supporters at L'Oréal include (in alphabetical order) Vincent Arcin, Alex Bennett, Jacques Challes, Sophie Cloarec, Irène Garcia Turcan, Diane Hecquet, Maud Jullien, and Emma Shuttleworth. There are many other wonderful people at L'Oréal, including many of our former students, who provided insights and support and whom we wish to thank as well.

Beyond L'Oréal, we wish to thank our colleagues at ESCP Business School, including Dean Frank Bournois, for their friendship and support. Marie Taillard extends her own thanks to Dean of Faculty Valérie Moatti, UK Dean Simon Mercado, and all her faculty colleagues in London for their continued friendship and encouragement, for giving her quality time to write the book proposal during her sabbatical year, and for inspiring her daily in her teaching and research. Béatrice is also very grateful to her colleagues at ESCP Business School on the Paris campus and elsewhere who have supported her in her sometimes complex moments and who have always been able to show her their support and friendship.

Several people helped the book see the light of day. Both authors are hugely grateful to their editor, Susan Lauzau, who understood what they wanted to write from the very early days, and helped immensely in translating their ambition into the book you are holding. John Willig, our agent, believed in the project and helped shepherd it into the hands of Jeannene Ray at Wiley. We are grateful to both.

On the personal front, the authors each owe a deep debt of gratitude to several people around them. Writing a book such as this one is demanding not just for the authors but for the people around them who give them the time and breathing room to focus and write. Marie wants to thank her husband, Joe, as well as her daughter, Emilie, and son, Thomas, who supported her throughout with their encouragement and by giving her time and space to write. Marie also would like to thank all her students, past and present, for inspiring her daily to think about so many of the topics in the book. Many former students will recognize arguments, examples, and terminology from class. This book would not have been possible without the many discussions, insights, and inspiration they provide daily. Béatrice is deeply grateful to her family—her husband, Jean-François, with whom she also shares her saga with L'Oréal, and her children, Clara and Thibaud, who have always been supportive and encouraging. Béatrice also has a special thought for the Necker team that has supported and accompanied her this past year. May everyone here be deeply thanked.

Finally, please note that the authors have agreed to list their names alphabetically.

About the Authors

Béatrice Collin

Béatrice Collin is Professor of Strategy and International Management at ESCP Business School, where she was Dean of the Faculty from 2014 to 2017. She has also taught at the University of Paris II and has been Visiting Professor at Cornell University (U.S.) and City University (UK). Since 2016, Collin has been a member of the Board of Directors of the École des Arts et Métiers Paris Tech (ENSAM).

Her teaching and research focus on international companies, their strategy, their governance, and their distinctive management issues, particularly in relation to cultural diversity. Collin works with large and medium-sized companies that are successfully leading their globalization process. She has also developed a recognized expertise in digital innovation and transformation, topics on which she regularly lectures in executive seminars. She has recently created a series of online modules on digital transformation for executives of large European and international firms looking for the key elements of reflection and action to succeed in the new digital age.

For more than twenty-five years, Collin has designed and run executive seminars for international companies interested in preparing their leaders (and future leaders) for the major changes and challenges of today's—and tomorrow's—world, be it digitalization, multipolarity, or the circular and sustainable economy.

With a triple specialty in management, international economics, and political science, Collin is a graduate of the Institut d'Études Politiques de Paris and completed her doctoral studies jointly with the Department of Economics and the Johnson Graduate School of Management at Cornell University, New York. She is a member, reviewer, and session chairperson of the Academy of Management, a member of EIASM (European Institute for Advanced Studies in Management), and a founding member of EURAM (European Academy of Management). In 2017, Collin received the insignia of "Chevalier de l'Ordre National du Mérite" from the French government.

Béatrice Collin has worked with and studied L'Oréal for many years. Her relationship with L'Oréal led to her book, coauthored in 2009 with Daniel Rouach, *Le Modèle L'Oréal,* in which she explored the key strategies of the French multinational company.

On the heels of the book's success, Collin has become a media expert on L'Oréal. She has given dozens of interviews in the French (print, radio, and television) and international media (BBC, *The Guardian, La Tribune de Genève, The International Herald Tribune*, and more) and contributed to various documentaries on L'Oréal. These opportunities led her to the idea for a second book, coauthored with Jean-François Delplancke and published by Dunod in 2015, *L'Oréal, la beauté de la stratégie*. The book was launched at ESCP Europe in the presence of L'Oréal CEO Jean-Paul Agon and other Executive Committee members.

Over more than twenty-five years, Beatrice Collin has built an in-depth knowledge of L'Oréal, its evolution, strategy, and identity, by forging strong links with the management teams while maintaining the objective stance of a researcher and observer.

Marie Taillard

Marie Taillard is a French-American senior marketing academic and business leader with more than thirty years of experience working at and consulting to small and large companies worldwide, teaching graduate business students, and leading learning and development programs for executives and senior executives (LVMH, Orange, 3M, Novartis, Lego, and more).

She is a faculty member at ESCP Business School, where she is tenured as a full-time Professor of Marketing. She sits on the School's European Faculty Advisory Board and is Head of Faculty for the London Campus of ESCP. She was previously a member of the School's European Teaching and Learning Committee.

Taillard developed Creativity Marketing, a new approach that emphasizes the need to adopt a more creative yet evidence-based approach to marketing in the context of digitalization and globalization. At ESCP she designed, launched, and managed two master's degrees (one full time, one part time for executives) in Creativity Marketing (ranked fifth worldwide among masters in marketing in 2018), and directs the Creativity Marketing Centre. She was named L'Oréal Professor of Creativity Marketing in 2015.

Taillard has previously lived in Australia, France, and the United States. A native speaker of French and English, she received a BA and an MA in Linguistics from the University of Southern California, an MBA from Columbia University's Graduate School of Business, and a PhD in Linguistics from the University of London (University College London).

She publishes in academic and managerial journals, including in the *Journal of Business Research* and *Harvard Business Review*, and presents her research at international marketing and management academic conferences. Much of her research is informed by her background as a manager and marketer, her multicultural experience, and her academic expertise in language, marketing, and creativity in organizations. These combined domains have also led to the development of an expertise in the challenges and opportunities linked to digital transformation.

Taillard also has an executive coaching practice and is certified as a senior practitioner by the European Mentoring and Coaching Council through the Tavistock Centre in London. She specializes in coaching senior executives whose organizations are undergoing digital transformations.

Before becoming an academic, Marie Taillard had a career as a marketer in the travel industry, including years spent at American Express and Council Travel as Vice President of Marketing and Product Development.

Appendix 1:
L'Oréal's History:
A Timeline of
Significant Dates

1909	La Société Française des Teintures Inoffensives pour Cheveux, later known as L'Oréal (1919), founded by Eugène Schueller
1928	Monsavon acquired
1936	Ambre Solaire sun care launched
1957	Françoise Dalle named CEO
1957	Monsavon sold to Procter & Gamble
1964	Lancôme acquired
1973	Synthélabo acquired
1974	Governance agreement finalized with Nestlé
1984	Charles Zviak named CEO
1985	Ralph Lauren (Warner Cosmetics) acquired
1988	Lindsay Owen-Jones named CEO
1994	L'Oréal USA incorporated
1994	L'Oréal subsidiary established in India
1996	Maybelline acquired
1997	L'Oréal subsidiary established in China
1998	Nihon L'Oréal incorporated
2003	Shu Uemara acquired
2006	Jean-Paul Agon named CEO
2010	Designated "The Digital Year" by Jean-Paul Agon
2011	New Lancôme mascara launched with animated teaser film and app

2011	Annual report includes a chapter on digital projects for the first time
2012	eSkin launched in China with an information and advice platform
2012	CBI (L'Oréal incubator) established
2012	Partnership agreement made with Tmall
2013	Lancôme lipstick launched in China using social media
2013	Partnership with YouTube celebrity Michelle Phan launched
2014	Makeup Genius virtual app released
2014	Partnership with YouTuber Michelle Phan dissolved
2014	Lubomira Rochet named CDO
2015	Style My Hair color try-on virtual makeover tool launched at hair salons
2016	Lancôme custom makeup Le Teint Particulier launched
2017	Ban the Boring campaign for Lancôme lipstick launched
2017	Simplicity manifesto unveiled
2018	Data sharing and customers campaign launched in China with Tmall
2019	#ColourMe virtual makeup try-on launched on Watsons app
2019	SkinConsult app launched by Vichy
2019	Lancôme flagship store opened in Paris
2020	Hairdressing and entrepreneurship bachelor's degree program inaugurated
2020	Eva Longoria's home video covering gray roots during COVID-19 lockdown released

Appendix 2: Timeline of L'Oréal's Acquisitions and Strategies

Brand	Acquisition Year	Country	Main Strategy
Monsavon*	1928	FRANCE	Entering body care and in-store retailing
Lancôme	1964	FRANCE	Entering into luxury products and retail
Garnier	1965	FRANCE	Entering cosmetics industry and strengthening mass-market hair products
Biotherm	1971	FRANCE	Entering into health care professionals' retailing networks
Synthélabo	1973	FRANCE	Entering pharmaceuticals industry
Vichy	1980	FRANCE	Strengthening health care professionals' retailing networks
Ralph Lauren (Warner Cosmetics)	1985	U.S.	Strengthening luxury perfumes and presence in the American market
Giorgio Armani	1985	ITALY	Strengthening luxury perfumes
Helena Rubinstein	1988	U.S.	Strengthening luxury products and presence in the American market

Brand	Acquisition Year	Country	Main Strategy
La Roche-Posay	1989	FRANCE	Strengthening health care professionals' retailing networks
Redken	1993	U.S.	Strengthening professional hairdressers' sales networks and presence in the American market
Maybelline	1996	U.S.	Developing mass-market makeup in the U.S., then worldwide
SoftSheen/Carson	1998/2000	U.S.	Developing ethnic skin and hair markets
Matrix	2000	U.S.	Strengthening professional hairdressers' sales networks and presence in the American market
Kiehl's	2000	US	Acquiring specific know-how in retailing and creativity in product design
Colorama	2001	BRAZIL	Strengthening Brazilian and South American mass markets
Shu Uemura	2003	JAPAN	Strengthening luxury products and presence in the Japanese market
Yue Sai	2004	CHINA	Accelerating growth in the mass-market segment in China
SkinCeuticals	2005	U.S.	Strengthening health care professionals' retailing networks and presence in the American market

Brand	Acquisition Year	Country	Main Strategy
Sanoflore	2006	FRANCE	Acquiring expertise on natural and organic products
The Body Shop**	2006	UK	Acquiring a new retail channel and expertise in ethical products
Roger & Gallet***	2008	FRANCE	Developing perfumes and soaps for health care professionals' retailing networks
Yves Saint Laurent	2010	FRANCE	Strengthening luxury products
Essie	2010	U.S.	Acquiring expertise in nail salons and nail polishes
Clarisonic****	2011	U.S.	Acquiring expertise in sonic technologies (brush)
Urban Decay	2012	U.S.	Acquiring expertise in assisted self-service sales and e-commerce
Vogue	2012	COLOMBIA	Strengthening presence in Central America and in South American Pacific Coast
Cheryl's Cosmeceuticals	2013	INDIA	Strengthening health care professionals' sales networks in India
Interbeauty Products	2013	KENYA	Local market knowledge and access to distribution channels
Emporio Body Store	2013	BRAZIL	Strengthening natural and ethical products sales in Brazil
Décléor/Carita	2014	FRANCE	Strengthening health care professionals' retailing networks

Brand	Acquisition Year	Country	Main Strategy
NYX Cosmetics	2014	U.S.	Acquiring expertise in digitalization and developing the "Make-up artist" trend
Magic Holdings	2014	CHINA	Strengthening in Chinese mass markets (facial masks)
Carol's Daughter	2014	U.S.	Developing natural products for the ethnic market
Niely Cosmeticos	2014	BRAZIL	Further learning about hair diversity
It Cosmetics	2016	U.S.	Developing products combining skincare and makeup
Atelier Cologne	2016	FRANCE	Entering niche perfumery and exclusive fragrances
St Gervais Mont Blanc	2016	FRANCE	Expanding in affordable dermo-cosmetics and sales development in spas
CeraVe	2017	U.S.	Expanding in affordable dermo-cosmetics and strengthening presence in the U.S. market
Logocos	2018	GERMANY	Developing organic and vegan cosmetics
ModiFace	2018	CANADA	Acquiring AI/AR Competencies
Stylenanda	2018	KOREA	Developing in K-beauty (Korean beauty)
Pulp Riot	2018	U.S.	Acquiring expertise in digitalization and strengthening professional hairdresser sales networks

Brand	Acquisition Year	Country	Main Strategy
Valentino	2018	ITALY	Strengthening in the luxury market
Mugler and Azzaro Fragrances	2020	FRANCE	Strengthening luxury perfumes
Thayers Natural Remedies	2020	U.S.	Strengthening natural products in the mass skin care market

* Sold to Procter & Gamble (USA) in 1960
** Sold to Natura Cosmeticos (Brazil) in 2017
*** Sold to Impala Holding (France) in 2020
**** Shut down in 2020

Appendix 3: A Selection of L'Oréal Brands by Category 2020

CONSUMER PRODUCTS

L'ORÉAL PARIS · MAYBELLINE NEW YORK · essie · NYX PROFESSIONAL MAKEUP

L'ORÈAL LUXE

ARMANI · Atelier Cologne · DIESEL · it COSMETICS · shu uemura · VALENTINO · YUESAI

PROFESSIONAL PRODUCTS

KÉRASTASE PARIS · MATRIX · PUREOLOGY serious colour care

ACTIVE COSMETICS

 CeraVe · SkinCeuticals ADVANCED PROFESSIONAL SKINCARE · VICHY LABORATOIRES

Appendix 4: Global Beauty Industry Data

Global Cosmetics Market

	2010	2011	2012	2013	2014	2015	2016	2017	2018	2019
Estimated like-for-like sales growth (%)	4.2	4.6	4.6	3.8	3.6	3.9	4	4.5	5.5	5.5
Breakdown by geographic zone (% of total sales)										
Asia Pacific	30	31	34	33	35	36	37	37	39	41
North America	22	20	21	22	21	24	25	25	25	24
Western Europe	26	24	22	22	22	20	19	18	18	18
Latin America	11	13	12	13	12	11	10	11	9	8
Eastern Europe	8	9	7	8	7	6	6	6	6	6
Africa, Middle East	3	3	4	3	3	3	3	3	3	3
Breakdown by business segments (% of total sales)										
Skincare	32	31	34	34	35	36	36	37	39	40
Haircare	26	25	25	24	23	23	23	22	21	21
Make-up	16	17	16	17	16	17	18	19	19	18
Fragrances	13	14	13	13	13	12	12	12	11	11
Hygiene products	12	12	11	11	11	11	11	10	10	10
Share of e-commerce (% total sales)					5	6	11	10	12.5	14

Main Worldwide Players (Total sales in Bn US$)

	2010	2011	2012	2013	2014	2015	2016	2017	2018	2019
L'Oréal	24.3	25.8	28.3	28.8	30.5	29.9	28	28.6	29.4	31.8
Unilever	15.3	16.9	18.5	20.7	21.3	21.6	20.4	20.5	21.5	22.4
Estée Lauder	7.9	8.2	9.4	9.9	10.3	10.9	17.6	15.4	12.4	13.2
Procter & Gamble	18.6	19.5	20.7	20.0	20.5	19.8	17.6	15.4	12.4	13.2
Shiseido	7.1	7.7	8.5	8.3	7.7	7.3	7.1	7.7	8.8	9.7
Coty	3.4	4.0	4.6	4.6	4.5	4.3	4.3	5.4	9.2	9.1

L'Oréal

	2010	2011	2012	2013	2014	2015	2016	2017	2018	2019
Total sales (Bn €)	19.5	20.3	22.4	22.9	22.5	25.2	25.8	26	26.9	29.8
Like-for-like sales growth	5.6	5.1	5.5	5	3.7	12.1	4.7	4.8	7.1	8
E-commerce										
Total sales (Bn €)						1.3	1.7	2.1	3	4.6
% Total sales						5.2	6.5	8	11	15.6
Like-for-like sales growth						37.9	32.7	33.6	40.6	52.4

(continued)

	2010	2011	2012	2013	2014	2015	2016	2017	2018	2019
% Total sales by division										
Consumer products	52.5	52.1	51.5	51	49.7	48.7	48.1	46.6	44.7	42.7
Luxury products	24.9	25.5	26.8	27.5	28.6	29.8	30.8	32.5	34.8	36.9
Professional products	15.0	14.9	14.4	14	14	14	13.6	12.9	12.1	11.5
Active cosmetics	7.6	7.5	7.3	7.5	7.7	7.5	7.5	8	8.4	8.9
% Total sales by geographic zone										
Western Europe	39.6	38.4	35.6	35.1	35.5	33.1	32.1	31.2	29.9	27.7
North America	23.6	23.3	25	25.1	24.9	27.4	28.5	28.3	26.9	25.3
Asia Pacific	17.6	19.2	20.6	20.6	21.1	22.5	22.6	23.6	27.5	32.3
Eastern Europe	7.7	7.1	6.8	7.9	7.3	6.3	6.3	6.7	6.5	6.4
Latin America	8.4	8.9	8.8	8.9	8.6	7.7	7.4	7.5	6.6	6
Africa, Middle East	3.1	3.1	3.3	2.4	2.6	3	3.1	2.7	2.6	2.3
% Total sales by business segments										
Skincare and sun protection	27.2	27.9	29.1	29.7	30	29.6	28.5	29.3	31.8	35
Make-up	21.2	21.5	21.5	21.7	21.9	23.8	26.4	27.9	27.4	26.3
Haircare	22.1	21.3	21	20.7	20.5	19.7	19.2	17.5	16.2	14.9
Hair coloring	15.0	14.6	14.1	13.8	13.2	12.7	12.1	11.8	10.9	10.1
Fragrances	10.0	9.8	9.7	9.5	9.8	9.8	99.5	9.2	9.3	9.3
Others	4.5	4.9	4.6	4.6	4.6	4.4	4.4	4.3	4.4	4.4

	2010	2011	2012	2013	2014	2015	2016	2017	2018	2019
Operating Profit (in Bn€)	2.9	3.2	3.7	3.8	3.9	4.3	4.5	4.6	4.9	5.5
Operating margin (% Total sales)	15.7	16.2	16.5	16.9	17.3	17.4	17.6	18	18.3	18.6
Net profit (in Bn€)	2.3	2.5	2.9	3.1	3.1	3.5	3.6	3.7	3.9	4.3
Capital expenditure (% Total sales)	3.5	4.3	4.3	4.6	4.5	4.6	5.4	4.9	5.3	4.1
Net cash surplus (in Bn€)	0.5	0.5	1.5	0.2	0.5	0.6	0.4	1.8	2.7	2.4
Share price (in €)	83.0	80.7	104.9	127.7	139.3	155.3	173.4	184.9	201.2	264
Market capitalization (in Bn €)	49.93	48.66	63.86	77.37	78.18	87.4	97.4	103.7	112.7	147.3

Notes

Introduction

1. The term "lipstick effect" was coined in 2008 by Leonard Lauder, former chairman of Estée Lauder.
2. Jay DiMartino, "What Skills Do You Need to Be a Good Surfer?" Liveaboutdotcom, Dotdash, May 28, 2018, https://www.liveabout.com/skills-needed-to-be-a-good-surfer-3154812.
3. Cecile Le Coz and François Monnier, "Le digital est pour nous un avantage compétitif (Digital is a competitive advantage for us)," *Investir*, Les Echos, May 18, 2019, https://investir.lesechos.fr/actionnaires/interview/le-digital-est-pour-nous-un-avantage-competitif-1849642.php.
4. Joseph A. Schumpeter, *Capitalism, Socialism, and Democracy* (New York: Harper and Row, 1976; originally published 1942), 132.

Chapter 1

1. Erin Griffith, "Why L'Oréal's CEO Loves 'Organized Chaos,'" *Fortune,* March 15, 2017, https://fortune.com/2017/03/15/loreal-ceo-jean-paul-agon/.
2. Aileen Ionescu-Somers and Albrecht Enders, "How Nestlé Dealt with a Social Media Campaign Against It," *Financial Times,* December 3, 2012.
3. Jack Neff, "L'Oréal Hikes Digital Ad Spend Sharply as Focus Shifts," *AdAge,* October 6, 2011, https://adage.com/article/media/l-oreal-hikes-digital-ad-spend-sharply-focus-shifts/230276.
4. *L'Oréal Annual Report, 2010,* 8, https://www.loreal-finance.com/_docs/us/2010-annual-report/LOREAL-2010-AR-volume1DEF.pdf.

5. L'Oréal sold Body Shop in 2017 to Natura Cosmeticos of Brazil.
6. Griffith, "Organized Chaos."
7. Frank Barrett, "What Leaders Can Learn from Jazz," interview by Jeff Kehoe, HBR IdeaCast from *Harvard Business Review,* August 29, 2012, Episode 316, https://hbr.org/podcast/2012/08/what-leaders-can-learn-from-ja.
8. Stephen Hebron, "John Keats and Negative Capability," *Discovering Literature, Romantics and Victorians,* British Library, May 15, 2014, https://www.bl.uk/romantics-and-victorians/articles/john-keats-and-negative-capability.
9. *L'Oréal Annual Report, 2011,* 75, https://www.loreal-finance.com/_docs/us/2011-annual-report/LOREAL_Rapport-Activite-2011.pdf.
10. Gaëlle Fleitour, "Google ne peut pas tuer L'Oréal, au contraire! (Google can't kill L'Oréal, on the contrary!)," *L'Usine Nouvelle,* September 25, 2014, 34.
11. Corinne Bouchouchi, "L'étoile Tech des cosmétiques (The Tech Star of Cosmetics)," *L'Obs,* April 5, 2018, 50.
12. Maria Grazia Meda, "Lubomira Rochet: je vois le digital comme une révolution industrielle (Lubomira Rochet: I see digital as an industrial revolution,)," *Le Figaro,* October 6, 2016, http://madame.lefigaro.fr/business/lubomira-rochet-je-vois-le-digital-comme-une-revolution-industr-061016-117121.
13. Bouchouchi, "The Tech Star," 50.
14. Julien Dupont-Calbo, "Moi, Chief Digital Officer (I, Chief Digital Officer)," *Les Échos,* April 13, 2016, 13.
15. Emmanuelle Delsol, "Profession CDO: Lubomira Rochet prône un management frugal pour la transformation digitale de L'Oréal (CDO Profession: Lubomira Rochet advocates frugal management for the digital transformation of L'Oréal)," *L'Usine Nouvelle,* February 17, 2015, https://www.usine-digitale.fr/article/profession-cdo-lubomira-rochet-prone-un-management-frugal-pour-la-transformation-digitale-de-l-oreal.N304290.
16. Delsol, "Profession CDO."
17. Fleitour, "Google," 34.

Chapter 2

1. Molly Fleming, L'Oréal CMO: Companies That Just Sell Products Will Not Be Successful," *Marketing Week,* October 19, 2018, https://www.marketingweek.com/loreal-services/.

2. Mirabelle Belloir, "La disruption est stimulante pour Jean-Paul Agon, le pdg de L'Oréal (Disruption is stimulating for Jean-Paul Agon, CEO of L'Oréal)," *LSA*, November 27, 2019, https://www.lsa-conso.fr/lsa-live-la-disruption-est-stimulante-pour-jean-paul-agon-le-pdg-de-l-oreal,334381.

3. François Dalle, *L' Aventure L'Oréal (L'Oréal Adventure)* (Paris: Editions Odile Jacob, 2001), 286.

4. In Béatrice Collin and Jean-François Delplancke, *L'Oréal, la beauté de la stratégie (L'Oréal, the Beauty of Strategy)*, (Paris: Dunod, 2015), 48.

5. In Collin, L'Oréal, 48.

6. Ivan Letessier, "La lotion digitale de L'Oréal pour se transformer en BeautyTech (L'Oréal's digital lotion to become BeautyTech)," *Le Figaro*, December 2, 2019, https://www.lefigaro.fr/societes/la-lotion-digitale-de-l-oreal-pour-se-transformer-en-beautytech-20191201.

7. Pete Born, "Visionary of The Year: Jean-Paul Agon of L'Oréal," *WWD*, December 1, 2015, https://wwd.com/business-news/human-resources/visionary-of-the-year-jean-paul-agon-loreal-10292231/.

8. Erin Griffith, "Why L'Oréal's CEO Loves 'Organized Chaos," *Fortune*, March 15, 2017, https://fortune.com/2017/03/15/loreal-ceo-jean-paul-agon/.

9. Dalle, *L' Aventure L'Oréal.*

10. Lene Constanty, Barraux Jacques, and Gérard Moatti, Lindsay Owen-Jones, Marchand de beauté (Lindsay Owen-Jones, Beauty Merchant), *L'expansion*, April 16, 1992, https://lexpansion.lexpress.fr/actualite-economique/lindsay-owen-jones-marchand-de-beaute_1369863.html.

11. Jean-Paul Agon, interviewed by Beatrice Collin and Jean-François Delplancke, January 17, 2013.

12. Bruna Basini, "Les Secrets d'un grand fauve (The Secrets of a Great Tiger)," *L'Express*, December 1, 2002, https://lexpansion.lexpress.fr/actualite-economique/les-secrets-d-un-grand-fauve_1338898.html.

13. Frédéric Rozé, interviewed by Beatrice Collin and Jean-François Delplancke, November 28, 2012.

14. Letessier, "La lotion digitale."

15. Jean-Paul Agon, interviewed by Tania Bryer, *The CNBC Conversation*, January 5, 2015.

16. *L'Oréal Annual Report, 2017,* https://www.loreal-finance.com/en/annual-report-2017/worldwide-advances/china.

17. Hal Sirkin, Jim Hemerling, and Arindam Bhattacharya, *Globality: Competing with Everyone from Everywhere for Everything* (London: Headline, 2012).

18. Lucy Handley, "The World's Largest Beauty Company Sees China as Its Digital 'Laboratory,'" *CNBC*, September 3, 2019, https://www.cnbc.com/2019/09/03/how-loreal-uses-china-as-a-place-to-learn-about-digital-marketing.html.

19. Dalle, *L' Aventure L'Oréal, 83.*

20. Lubomira Rochet, interviewed by Beatrice Collin and Marie Taillard, November 21, 2018.

Chapter 3

1. Julian Birkinshaw, Jean-Louis Barsoux, and Cyril Bouquet, "The 5 Myths of Innovation," *MIT Sloan Management Review*, 52, 2011, 43–50.

2. Fleitour Gaëlle and Thibaut de Jaegher, "Google ne peut pas tuer L'Oréal (Google can't kill L'Oréal)," *L'Usine Nouvelle*, September 23, 2014, https://www.usine-digitale.fr/article/jean-paul-agon-google-ne-peut-pas-tuer-l-oreal-au-contraire.N285733.

3. François Dalle, *L' Aventure L'Oréal (L'Oréal Adventure)* (Paris: Editions Odile Jacob, 2001), 290.

4. Ibid.

5. Jean-Paul Agon, "Leaders with Lacqua," interviewed by Francine Lacqua, Bloomberg TV, December 27, 2017, https://www.bloomberg.com/news/videos/2017-12-29/leaders-with-lacqua-l-oreal-ceo-jean-paul-agon-video.

6. Bruna Basini, "Les Secrets d'un grand fauve (The Secrets of a Great Tiger)," *L'Express*, December 1, 2002, https://lexpansion.lexpress.fr/actualite-economique/les-secrets-d-un-grand-fauve_1338898.html.

7. Richard C. Morais, "The Color of Beauty," *Forbes*, November 27, 2000, https://www.forbes.com/forbes/2000/1127/6614170a.html#5474dcff51ec.

8. Geoffrey Moore, *Crossing the Chasm*, 3rd ed. (New York: Collins Business Essentials, Harper Business, 2014).

9. Harriet Agnew and Scheherazade Daneshkhu, "L'Oréal Success Story Goes Deep Below the Skin," *Financial Times,* June 30, 2017, https://www.ft.com/content/ad0ed0ca-5cae-11e7-9bc8-8055f264aa8b.

10. Lubomira Rochet, interviewed by Beatrice Collin and Marie Taillard, November 21, 2018.

11. Leila Abboud, "L'Oréal Glimpses Its Digital Future Amid Pandemic," *Financial Times*, June 15, 2020, https://www.ft.com/content/ab917d5d-e601-44ba-9a2c-53dbb2146dc7.

Chapter 4

1. Barbara Santamaria, "L'Oréal Launches AI-Powered Digital Skin Diagnostic," *Fashion Network*, February 19, 2019, https://www.fashionnetwork.com/news/L-oreal-launches-ai-powered-digital-skin-diagnostic,1069850.html.
2. Jacques Marseille, *L'Oréal 1909–2009* (Paris: Perrin, 2009), 205.
3. Gail Edmondson, "L'Oréal: The Beauty of Global Branding," Bloomberg, June 28, 1999, https://www.bloomberg.com/news/articles/1999-06-27/loreal-the-beauty-of-global-branding-intl-edition.
4. *L'Oréal Annual Report, 2016,* https://www.loreal-finance.com/en/annual-report-2016/mission-strategy.
5. Ivan Letessier, "Alibaba accélère la croissance de L'Oréal en Chine (Alibaba accelerates L'Oréal's growth in China)," *Le Figaro*, March 12, 2018, 26.
6. L'Oréal, "Winning through Consumer Obsession," *L'Oréal Chine CMD 2018*, 2018, https://www.loreal-finance.com/system/files/2019-08/CMD_2018_LOreal_Chine.pdf.
7. Liz Flora, "Brands Now Support Black Lives Matter but They Used to Avoid Influencers That Did the Same," *Glossy.co*, June 11, 2020, https://www.glossy.co/beauty/brands-now-support-black-lives-matter-but-they-used-to-avoid-influencers-that-did-the-same.
8. Thomson Reuters, "Thomson Reuters DI Index Ranks the 2018 Top 100 Most Diverse and Inclusive Organizations Globally," September 6, 2018, https://www.thomsonreuters.com/en/press-releases/2018/september/thomson-reuters-di-index-ranks-the-2018-top-100-most-diverse-and-inclusive-organizations-globally.html.
9. Jenna Ammann, "L'Oréal Advertises Gender Diversity 'Because Women Are Worth It,'" *Triple Pundit*, April 12, 2019, https://www.triplepundit.com/story/2019/loreal-advertises-gender-diversity-because-women-are-worth-it/83146/.
10. Edmondson, "Global Branding."
11. Geoffrey G. Jones, David Kiron, Vincent Dessain, and Anders Sjoman, "L'Oréal and the Globalization of the American Beauty," *HBS Case Study*, HBS Case Collection, April 2005, Revised February 2006.

12. Sara Castellanos, "How L'Oréal Expands Virtual Try-On Service," *Wall Street Journal,* December 19, 2019, https://www.wsj.com/articles/ loreal-expands-virtual-try-on-service-11576776586.

13. Vincent Arcin, Global Digital Services Director, Conference Presentation, ESCP BS, Paris Campus, October 1, 2018.

Chapter 5

1. The notion of a customer's "job-to-be-done" was developed by the late Clayton Christensen, a Harvard Business School academic and consultant in a number of articles and in the book *Competing Against Luck: The Story of Innovation and Customer Choice* (HarperCollins, 2016). It is also associated with human-centered innovation methodologies such as design thinking and with the Business Model Canvas approach of Alexander Osterwalder and Yves Pigneur.

2. This is the Persuasion Knowledge Model theory of consumer behavior developed by Marian Friestad and Peter Wright in their 1994 *Journal of Consumer Research* article "The Persuasion Knowledge Model: How People Cope with Persuasion Attempts." The "model" is the mental model individuals have of what it takes to persuade or be persuaded, rather than the name of the theory.

3. Stéphane Bérubé, "Never Stop Learning: Why Staying Ahead of Marketing Matters Today," *Think With Google,* October 2018, https:// www.thinkwithgoogle.com/intl/en-154/insights-inspiration/ thought-leadership/future-marketers-why-staying-ahead- marketing-matters-today/.

4. Molly Fleming, "L'Oréal CMO: Companies That Just Sell Products Will Not Be Successful," *Marketing Week*, October 19, 2018, https://www .marketingweek.com/loreal-services/.

5. AFP-Relaxnews, "La cosmétique à l'ère de l'hyper personnalisation (Cosmetics in the age of hyper-customization)," *Fashion Network*, December 27, 2018, https://fr.fashionnetwork.com/news/La-cosmetique-a- l-ere-de-l-hyper-personnalisation,1047953.html.

6. Cookies are text files included in websites and online ads that are downloaded onto a user's computer to track data about the user's use of the site and shared back with the publisher or advertiser. They allow publishers and advertisers to target users more effectively.

7. Jacques Marseille, *L'Oréal 1909–2009* (Paris: Perrin, 2009), 152.

8. Nicholas Confessore, "Cambridge Analytica and Facebook: The Scandal and the Fallout So Far," *New York Times,* April 4, 2018, https://www.nytimes

.com/2018/04/04/us/politics/cambridge-analytica-scandal-fallout.html.

9. Harry Englar, "Ethics Is Key to Filling Growing Gap as Technology Outpaces Regulation—L'Oreal Chief Ethics Officer," *Thomson Reuters Regulatory Intelligence blog*, Thomson Reuters, June 6, 2019, https://blogs.thomsonreuters.com/answerson/ethics-technology-regulation-loreal/.

Chapter 6

1. Militza Yovanka, "Perfect Eyebrow Tutorial + How to Fix a MicroBlading Fail," YouTube video, October 17, 2017, https://www.youtube.com/watch?v=hITtcFAXhYc; Militza Yovanka, "How to Achieve Blue Hair with L'Oréal Colorista," YouTube video, May 25, 2018, https://www.youtube.com/watch?v=R3XzTPHNpMA; Militza Yovanka, "Current Favorites + Products That Bring Comfort," YouTube video, April 22, 2020, https://www.youtube.com/watch?v=eS-Mm5eSN48.

2. Craig J. Thompson and Elizabeth C. Hirschman, "Understanding the Socialized Body: A Poststructuralist Analysis of Consumers' Self-Conceptions, Body Images, and Self-Care Practices," *Journal of Consumer Research* 22, no. 2 (1995): 139–153.

3. Erving Goffman, *The Presentation of Self in Everyday Life* (New York: Doubleday, 1959).

4. Trudy Hui Hui Chua and Leanne Chang, "Follow Me and Like My Beautiful Selfies: Singapore Teenage Girls' Engagement in Self-Presentation and Peer Comparison on Social Media," *Computers in Human Behavior* 55 (2016): 190–197.

5. Yovanka, "Current Favorites."

6. Emma Sandler, "My Role Is Changing: Mega-Influencer Pony on Working with Eastern and Western Beauty Brands," *Glossy*, January 21, 2020, https://www.glossy.co/beauty/my-role-is-changing-mega-influencer-pony-on-working-with-eastern-and-western-beauty-brands.

7. Nitasha Tiku, "Inside Glossier, the Beauty Startup That Reached Cult Status by Selling Less," *BuzzFeed News*, August 25, 2016, https://www.buzzfeednews.com/article/nitashatiku/inside-glossier-the-beauty-startup-that-just-happens-to-sell.

8. Jill Avery, "Glossier: Co-Creating a Cult Brand with a Digital Community," Harvard Business School Publishing, October 22, 2019.

Chapter 7

1. James F. Moore, "Predators and Prey: A New Ecology of Competition," *Harvard Business Review*, May/June 1993, https://hbr.org/1993/05/predators-and-prey-a-new-ecology-of-competition.
2. Marco Iansiti and Roy Levien, *The Keystone Advantage: What the New Dynamics of Business Ecosystems Mean for Strategy, Innovation, and Sustainability* (Boston: Harvard Business School Press, 2004), 225.
3. Marie Taillard, Linda D. Peters, Jaqueline Pels, and Cristina Mele, "The Role of Shared Intentions in the Emergence of Service Ecosystems," *Journal of Business Research* 69, no. 8 (August 2016): 2972–2980, https://nottingham-repository.worktribe.com/output/806854/the-role-of-shared-intentions-in-the-emergence-of-service-ecosystems.
4. Gideon Spanier, "L'Oréal on the Media Agency of the Future and Being a Smarter Client," *Campaign*, June 27, 2019, https://www.campaignlive.co.uk/article/loreal-media-agency-future-smarter-client/1589065.
5. Spanier, "L'Oréal on the Media Agency."
6. Mirabelle Belloir, "La disruption est stimulante (Disruption is stimulating)," *LSA*, November 27, 2019, https://www.lsa-conso.fr/lsa-live-la-disruption-est-stimulante-pour-jean-paul-agon-le-pdg-de-l-oreal,334381.
7. Georgina Caldwell, "L'Oréal Q1 2020 E-commerce Saves the Day," *Global Cosmetics News*, April 20, 2020, https://www.globalcosmeticsnews.com/loreal-q1-2020-e-commerce-saves-the-day-as-sales-down-4-8-percent/.
8. Leila Abboud, "L'Oréal Glimpses Its Digital Future Amid Pandemic," *Financial Times*, June 15, 2020, https://www.ft.com/content/ab917d5d-e601-44ba-9a2c-53dbb2146dc7.

Chapter 8

1. Isabelle Jouanneau, "L'Oréal, les secrets d'un empire de la cosmétique (L'Oréal, the secrets of a cosmetics empire)," Entreprendre.fr, February 19, 2020, https://www.entreprendre.fr/loreal-jean-paul-agon-secrets-empire-cosmetique/.
2. Nicolas Hieronimus, "Inclusion Demands Authenticity," interviewed on Eve Programme Blog, October 8, 2018, https://www.eveprogramme.com/en/38746/interview-nicolas-hieronimus/.

References

Abboud, Leila. "L'Oréal Glimpses Its Digital Future Amid Pandemic." *Financial Times,* June 15, 2020. https://www.ft.com/content/ab917d5d-e601-44ba-9a2c-53dbb2146dc7.

AFP-Relaxnews. "La cosmétique à l'ère de l'hyper personnalisation (Cosmetics in the age of hyper-customization)." *Fashion Network,* December 27, 2018. https://fr.fashionnetwork.com/news/La-cosmetique-a-l-ere-de-l-hyper-personnalisation,1047953.html.

Agnew, Harriet, and Scheherazade Daneshkhu. "L'Oréal Success Story Goes Deep Below the Skin." *Financial Times,* June 30, 2017. https://www.ft.com/content/ad0ed0ca-5cae-11e7-9bc8-8055f264aa8b.

Agon, Jean-Paul. "Leaders with Lacqua," interviewed by Francine Lacqua, *Bloomberg TV,* December 27, 2017. https://www.bloomberg.com/news/videos/2017-12-29/leaders-with-lacqua-l-oreal-ceo-jean-paul-agon-video.

Agon, Jean-Paul. Interviewed by Tania Bryer. *The CNBC Conversation,* CNBC, January 6, 2018.

Ammann, Jenna. "L'Oréal Advertises Gender Diversity 'Because Women Are Worth It.'" *Triple Pundit,* April 12, 2019. https://www.triplepundit.com/story/2019/loreal-advertises-gender-diversity-because-women-are-worth-it/83146/.

Arcin, Vincent. Conference Presentation. ESCP BS, Paris Campus, October 1, 2018.

Avery, Jill. "Glossier: Co-Creating a Cult Brand with a Digital Community." Harvard Business School Publishing, October 22, 2019.

Barrett, Frank. "What Leaders Can Learn from Jazz." Interview by Jeff Kehoe. HBR IdeaCast from *Harvard Business Review,* August 29, 2012, Episode 316.

Basini, Bruna. "Les Secrets d'un grand fauve (The Secrets of a Great Tiger)." *L'Express,* December 1, 2002. https://lexpansion.lexpress.fr/actualite-economique/les-secrets-d-un-grand-fauve_1338898.htmlhttps://hbr.org/podcast/2012/08/what-leaders-can-learn-from-ja.

Belloir, Mirabelle. "La disruption est stimulante pour Jean-Paul Agon, le pdg de L'Oréal (Disruption is stimulating for Jean-Paul Agon, CEO of L'Oréal)." *LSA,* November 27, 2019. https://www.lsa-conso.fr/lsa-live-la-disruption-est-stimulante-pour-jean-paul-agon-le-pdg-de-l-oreal,334381.

Bérubé, Stéphane. "Never Stop Learning, Why Staying Ahead of Marketing Matters Today." *Think With Google,* October 2018. https://www.thinkwithgoogle.com/intl/en-154/insights-inspiration/thought-leadership/future-marketers-why-staying-ahead-marketing-matters-today/.

Birkinshaw, Julian, Jean-Louis Barsoux, and Cyril Bouquet. "The 5 Myths of Innovation." *MIT Sloan Management Review,* 52 (2011) 43–50.

Born, Pete. "Visionary of The Year: Jean-Paul Agon of L'Oréal." *WWD,* December 1, 2015. https://wwd.com/business-news/human-resources/visionary-of-the-year-jean-paul-agon-loreal-10292231/.

Bouchouchi, Corinne. "L'étoile Tech des cosmétiques (The Tech Star of Cosmetics)." *L'Obs,* April 5, 2018.

Caldwell, Georgina. "L'Oréal Q1 2020 E-commerce Saves the Day." *Global Cosmetics News,* April 20, 2020. https://www.globalcosmeticsnews.com/loreal-q1-2020-e-commerce-saves-the-day-as-sales-down-4-8-percent/.

Castellanos, Sara. "How L'Oréal Expands Virtual Try-On Service." *Wall Street Journal,* December 19, 2019. https://www.wsj.com/articles/loreal-expands-virtual-try-on-service-11576776586.

Christensen, Clayton M. *The Innovator's Dilemma: When New Technologies Cause Great Firms to Fail.* Boston: Harvard Business Review Press, 2013.

Christensen, Clayton M., Taddy Hall, Karen Dillon, and David S. Duncan. *Competing Against Luck: The Story of Innovation and Customer Choice.* New York: Harper Business, 2016.

Chua, Trudy Hui Hui, and Leanne Chang. "Follow Me and Like My Beautiful Selfies: Singapore Teenage Girls' Engagement in Self-Presentation and Peer Comparison on Social Media." *Computers in Human Behavior* 55 (2016): 190–197.

Collin, Béatrice, and Jean-François Delplancke. *L'Oréal, la beauté de la stratégie (L'Oréal, the Beauty of Strategy).* Paris: Dunod, 2015.

Confessore, Nicholas. "Cambridge Analytica and Facebook: The Scandal and the Fallout So Far." *New York Times,* April 4, 2018. https://www.nytimes.com/2018/04/04/us/politics/cambridge-analytica-scandal-fallout.html.

Constanty, Lene, Jacques Barraux, and Gérard Moatti. "Lindsay Owen-Jones, Marchand de beauté (Lindsay Owen-Jones, Beauty Merchant)." *L'expansion,* April 16, 1992. https://lexpansion.lexpress.

fr/actualite-economique/lindsay-owen-jones-marchand-de-beaute_1369863.html.

Davenport, Thomas, and Jeanne Harris. *Competing on Analytics: Updated, with a New Introduction: The New Science of Winning*. Boston: Harvard Business Review Press, 2017.

Dalle, François. *L' Aventure L'Oréal (L'Oréal Adventure)*. Paris: Editions Odile Jacob, 2001.

Delsol, Emmanuelle. "Profession CDO: Lubomira Rochet prône un management frugal pour la transformation digitale de L'Oréal (CDO Profession: Lubomira Rochet advocates frugal management for the digital transformation of L'Oréal)." *L'Usine Nouvelle*, February 17, 2015. https://www.usine-digitale.fr/article/profession-cdo-lubomira-rochet-prone-un-management-frugal-pour-la-transformation-digitale-de-l-oreal.N304290.

DiMartino, Jay. "What Skills Do You Need to Be a Good Surfer?" *Liveabout-dotcom*, Dotdash, May 28, 2018. https://www.liveabout.com/skills-needed-to-be-a-good-surfer-3154812.

Doz, Yves L., Jose Santos, and Peter Williamson. *From Global to Metanational: How Companies Win in the Knowledge Economy*. Boston: Harvard Business Review Press, 2001.

Dupont-Calbo, Julien. "Moi, Chief Digital Officer (I, Chief Digital Officer)." *Les Échos*, April 13, 2016.

Edelman, David C., and Marc Singer. "Competing on Customer Journeys." *Harvard Business Review* 93, no. 11 (2015): 88–100.

Edmondson, Amy. *The Fearless Organization: Creating Psychological Safety in the Workplace*. Hoboken, NJ: John Wiley & Sons, 2018.

Edmondson, Gail. "L'Oréal: The Beauty of Global Branding." Bloomberg, June 28, 1999. https://www.bloomberg.com/news/articles/1999-06-27/loreal-the-beauty-of-global-branding-intl-edition.

Englar Harry. "Ethics Is Key to Filling Growing Gap as Technology Outpaces Regulation—L'Oreal Chief Ethics Officer." *Thomson Reuters Regulatory Intelligence blog*. Thomson Reuters, June 6, 2019. https://blogs.thomsonreuters.com/answerson/ethics-technology-regulation-loreal/.

Fleitour, Gaëlle, and Thibaut de Jaegher. "Google ne peut pas tuer L'Oréal, au contraire! (Google can't kill L'Oréal, on the contrary!)." *L'Usine Nouvelle*, September 23, 2014. https://www.usine-digitale.fr/article/jean-paul-agon-google-ne-peut-pas-tuer-l-oreal-au-contraire.N285733.

Fleming, Molly. "L'Oréal CMO: Companies That Just Sell Products Will Not Be Successful." *Marketing Week,* October 19, 2018. https://www.marketingweek.com/loreal-services/.

Flora, Liz. "Brands Now Support Black Lives Matter but They Used to Avoid Influencers That Did the Same." *Glossy.co*, June 11, 2020. https://www.glossy.co/beauty/brands-now-support-black-lives-matter-but-they-used-to-avoid-influencers-that-did-the-same.

Goffman, Erving. *The Presentation of Self in Everyday Life*. New York: Doubleday, 1959.

Griffith, Erin. "Why L'Oréal's CEO Loves 'Organized Chaos.'" *Fortune*, March 15, 2017. https://fortune.com/2017/03/15/loreal-ceo-jean-paul-agon/.

Gupta, Sunil. *Driving Digital Strategy: A Guide to Reimagining Your Business*. Boston: Harvard Business Review Press, 2018.

Handley Lucy. "The World's Largest Beauty Company Sees China as Its Digital Laboratory." CNBC, September 3, 2019. https://www.cnbc.com/2019/09/03/how-loreal-uses-china-as-a-place-to-learn-about-digital-marketing.html.

Hebron, Stephen. "John Keats and Negative Capability." *Discovering Literature, Romantics and Victorians*. British Library, May 15, 2014. https://www.bl.uk/romantics-and-victorians/articles/john-keats-and-negative-capability.

Hieronimus, Nicolas. "Inclusion Demands Authenticity." Interviewed on Eve Programme Blog. October 8, 2018. https://www.eveprogramme.com/en/38746/interview-nicolas-hieronimus/.

Hsieh, Tony. *Delivering Happiness: A Path to Profits, Passion, and Purpose*. New York: Grand Central Publishing, 2010.

Iansiti, Marco, and Roy Levien. *The Keystone Advantage: What the New Dynamics of Business Ecosystems Mean for Strategy, Innovation, and Sustainability*. Boston: Harvard Business School Press, 2004.

Iansiti, Marco, and Roy Levien. "Strategy as Ecology." *Harvard Business Review* 82, no. 3: 68–78, 2004.

Iansiti, Marco, and Karim R. Lakhani. *Competing in the Age of AI: Strategy and Leadership When Algorithms and Networks Run the World*. Boston: Harvard Business Review Press, 2020.

Ionescu-Somers, Aileen, and Albrecht Enders. "How Nestlé Dealt with a Social Media Campaign Against It." *Financial Times*, December 3, 2012.

Jones, Geoffrey. *Beauty Imagined: A History of the Global Beauty Industry*. Oxford University Press, 2010.

Jones, Geoffrey G., David Kiron, Vincent Dessain, and Anders Sjoman. "L'Oréal and the Globalization of the American Beauty." *HBS Case Study*, HBS Case Collection, April 2005, Revised February 2006.

Jouanneau, Isabelle. "L'Oréal, les secrets d'un empire de la cosmétique (L'Oréal, the secrets of a cosmetics empire)." *Entreprendre.fr*, February 19, 2020.

https://www.entreprendre.fr/loreal-jean-paul-agon-secrets-empire-cosmetique/.

Le Coz, Cecile, and François Monnier. "Le digital est pour nous un avantage compétitif (Digital is a competitive advantage for us.)" *Investir*. Les Echos, May 18, 2019, https://investir.lesechos.fr/actionnaires/interview/le-digital-est-pour-nous-un-avantage-competitif-1849642.php.

Letessier, Ivan. "Alibaba accélère la croissance de L'Oréal en Chine (Alibaba accelerates L'Oréal's growth in China)." *Le Figaro*, March 12, 2018, 26.

Letessier, Ivan. "La lotion digitale de L'Oréal pour se transformer en Beauty-Tech (L'Oréal's digital lotion to become BeautyTech)." *Le Figaro,* December 2, 2019. https://www.lefigaro.fr/societes/la-lotion-digitale-de-l-oreal-pour-se-transformer-en-beautytech-20191201.

L'Oréal. "Winning through Consumer Obsession." *L'Oréal Chine CMD 2018*, 2018. https://www.loreal-finance.com/system/files/2019-08/CMD_2018_LOreal_Chine.pdf.

L'Oréal Annual Report, 2010. https://www.loreal-finance.com/_docs/us/2010-annual-report/LOREAL-2010-AR-volume1DEF.pdf.

L'Oréal Annual Report, 2011. https://loreal-dam-front-corp-en-cdn.damdy.com/ressources/afile/2539-30db6-resource-l-oreal-2011-activity-report.html.

L'Oréal Annual Report, 2016. https://www.loreal-finance.com/en/annual-report-2016/mission-strategy.

L'Oréal Annual Report, 2017. https://www.loreal-finance.com/sites/default/files/2019-09/LOreal_Rapport_Annuel_2017.pdf

Marseille, Jacques. *L'Oréal 1909–2009.* Paris: Perrin, 2009.

Meda, Maria Grazia. "Lubomira Rochet: je vois le digital comme une révolution industrielle (Lubomira Rochet: I see digital as an industrial revolution)." *Le Figaro*, October 6, 2016. http://madame.lefigaro.fr/business/lubomira-rochet-je-vois-le-digital-comme-une-revolution-industr-061016-117121.

Moore, Geoffrey. *Crossing the Chasm*, 3rd ed. New York: Collins Business Essentials, Harper Business, 2014.

Moore, James F. "Predators and Prey: A New Ecology of Competition." *Harvard Business Review*, May/June 1993. https://hbr.org/1993/05/predators-and-prey-a-new-ecology-of-competition.

Morais, Richard C. "The Color of Beauty." *Forbes*, November 27, 2000. https://www.forbes.com/forbes/2000/1127/6614170a.html#5474dcff51ec.

Muñiz, Albert M., and Marie Taillard. "Co-Constructing Institutions One Brick at a Time: Appropriation and Deliberation on LEGO Ideas." In *The Routledge Companion to Consumer Behavior*, 422–441. Oxford, UK: Routledge, 2017.

Nadella, Satya. *Hit Refresh: The Quest to Rediscover Microsoft's Soul and Imagine a Better Future for Everyone*. New York: Harper Collins, 2017.

Neff, Jack. "L'Oréal Hikes Digital Ad Spend Sharply as Focus Shifts." *AdAge*, October 6, 2011. https://adage.com/article/media/l-oreal-hikes-digital-ad-spend-sharply-focus-shifts/230276.

Osterwalder, Alexander, and Yves Pigneur. *Business Model Generation: A Handbook for Visionaries, Game Changers, and Challengers*. Hoboken, NJ: John Wiley & Sons, 2010.

Pine, B. Joseph, and James H. Gilmore. *The Experience Economy*. Boston: Harvard Business Review Press, 2011.

Prahalad, Coimbatore Krishna, and Venkat Ramaswamy. *The Future of Competition: Co-creating Unique Value with Customers*. Boston: Harvard Business Review Press, 2004.

Reillier, Laure Claire, and Benoit Reillier. *Platform Strategy: How to Unlock the Power of Communities and Networks to Grow Your Business*. New York: Taylor & Francis, 2017.

Ries, Eric. *The Lean Start-Up*. New York: Currency/Penguin Random House, 2011.

Sandler, Emma. "My Role Is Changing: Mega-Influencer Pony on Working with Eastern and Western Beauty Brands." *Glossy*, January 21, 2020. https://www.glossy.co/beauty/my-role-is-changing-mega-influencer-pony-on-working-with-eastern-and-western-beauty-brands.

Santamaria, Barbara. "L'Oréal Launches AI-Powered Digital Skin Diagnostic." *Fashion Network*, February 19, 2019. https://www.fashionnetwork.com/news/L-oreal-launches-ai-powered-digital-skin-diagnostic,1069850.html.

Schau, Hope Jensen, Albert M. Muñiz Jr, and Eric J. Arnould. "How Brand Community Practices Create Value." *Journal of Marketing* 73, no. 5 (2009): 30–51.

Schumpeter, Joseph. *Capitalism, Socialism, and Democracy*. New York: Harper and Row, 1976; originally published 1942.

Sirkin, Hal, Jim Hemerling, and Arindam Bhattacharya. *Globality: Competing with Everyone from Everywhere for Everything*. London: Headline, 2012.

Slater, Stanley F., and John C. Narver. "Market Orientation and the Learning Organization." *Journal of Marketing* 59, no. 3 (1995): 63–74.

Spanier, Gideon. "L'Oréal on the Media Agency of the Future and Being a Smarter Client." *Campaign*, June 27, 2019. https://www.campaignlive.co.uk/article/loreal-media-agency-future-smarter-client/1589065.

Taillard, Marie, Linda D. Peters, Jaqueline Pels, and Cristina Mele. "The Role of Shared Intentions in the Emergence of Service Ecosystems." *Journal of Business Research* 69 no. 8 (August 2016): 2972–2980. https://nottingham-repository.worktribe.com/output/806854/the-role-of-shared-intentions-in-the-emergence-of-service-ecosystems.

Thompson, Craig J., and Elizabeth C. Hirschman, "Understanding the Socialized Body: A Poststructuralist Analysis of Consumers' Self-Conceptions, Body Images, and Self-Care Practices." *Journal of Consumer Research* 22, no. 2 (1995): 139–153.

Thomson Reuters. "Thomson Reuters DI Index Ranks the 2018 Top 100 Most Diverse and Inclusive Organizations Globally." September 6, 2018. https://www.thomsonreuters.com/en/press-releases/2018/september/thomson-reuters-di-index-ranks-the-2018-top-100-most-diverse-and-inclusive-organizations-globally.html.

Tiku, Nitasha. "Inside Glossier, the Beauty Startup That Reached Cult Status by Selling Less." *BuzzFeed News,* August 25, 2016. https://www.buzzfeednews.com/article/nitashatiku/inside-glossier-the-beauty-startup-that-just-happens-to-sell.

Tse, Terence C.M., Mark Esposito, and Danny Goh. *The AI Republic: Building the Nexus Between Humans and Intelligent Automation.* Austin, TX: Lioncrest Publishing, 2019.

Vargo, Stephen L., and Robert F. Lusch. "Service-Dominant Logic." In *The Service-Dominant Logic of Marketing: Dialog, Debate, and Directions,* ed. Stephen L. Vargo and Robert F. Lusch. New York: Taylor & Francis, 2006.

Verhoef, Peter, Edwin Kooge, and Natasha Walk. *Creating Value with Big Data Analytics: Making Smarter Marketing Decisions.* New York: Routledge, 2016.

Westerman, George, Didier Bonnet, and Andrew McAfee. "The Nine Elements of Digital Transformation." *MIT Sloan Management Review* 55, no. 3 (2014): 1–6.

Westerman, George, Didier Bonnet, and Andrew McAfee. *Leading Digital: Turning Technology into Business Transformation.* Boston: Harvard Business Review Press, 2014.

Index

A

Agon, Jean-Paul, 3–6, 8–9, 21–22, 28, 30, 40, 42–43, 58, 113, 120, 122–123
Alexandre de Paris, 55
Alibaba, 18, 66
Alignment, 129
Allianz, digital transformation, 14
Amazon, L'Oréal competition, 113
Amazon, Luxury Beauty Store, 11
Ambre Solaire, 25–26, 59
Armani (L'Oréal brand), 53, 62
Armani, Giorgio, 52
Arnal, Jacqueline/Maurice, 32
Artificial intelligence (AI), 27, 64, 82
Asos, 51
A.S. Watson (ASW), 66–67, 84, 115
Audacity, 42–43
Augmented reality (AR), 51–52, 64, 82
Autumn Moon Festival, 58

B

Baidu, Alibaba, Tencent (BAT), 31
Baidu, L'Oréal partnership, 66
Bakelite, 39
Balooch, Guive, 47–48
Beauty Gifter, 77
Beauty Tech Labs, 112
Beckham, David, 85
Benzyl salicylate, 25

Bergdorf, Munroe, 128
Bergson, Henri, 54
Bernstein, Matt, 116
Bérubé, Stéphane, 21, 78, 112
Big data, 3
Biotherm, 17
Black Naturals (Garnier), 57
Body Shop, The, 7, 24, 31, 63, 126
Boutiqaat , 66
Box concept (vending machine), 52
Brick-and-mortar retailers, 83
Business insights, 85–87
Business Opportunities for L'Oréal Development (BOLD), 65

C

Capabilities access, 111–112
Carol's Daughter, 60
Cathay Innovation, 65
Central Pharmacy of France, 38
CES (Consumer Electronics Show), 48–49
Challengers, 30–34
Chanel, digital transformation, 14
Change
  ease, 34
  management approach, 15
  opportunities, 21–22
  promoters, 47–50
Channels, 26, 62
Chief Digital Officer (CDO), 13–15

Chief Executive Officer (CEO),
  conviction, 5
China
  economy, acceleration, 58–59
  lockdown, 114–115
  L'Oréal market/operations,
    17, 30
  market, function, 18
  omnichannel approach, 18–19
  torture test, 58–59
Chinese New Year, 58
Citizen Day program, 127
Clarins, 28
Clarisonic, 44, 46, 126
Classes préparatoires, 123
"Clean children's crusade," Dop
  launch, 78
Clickstream data, 85
Collaboration, 120, 135–136
  shutdown, 25
  solution-focused collaboration
    (ecosystem attribute), 110–111
Color&Co, 45–46
ColourMe, 84
Competitive advantage, 59–60
Confrontation, 25, 135–136
Confrontation room, 24–25, 132
Connected Beauty Institute
  (CBI), 11–12
Consumer
  centricity, 7–8
  experience, 83–84
  insights, impact, 85
  jobs-to-be-done, 75, 85
  power, 29
  resistance, 76
Control, framing/trust, 128–130
Cookie-based marketing, 80–81
Cooperation, 25, 120, 121, 135–136
Corporate digital strategy, 16–17
Cosmair (Cosmetics for Hair), 55
COVID-19 pandemic, 29,
    32, 47, 74–75
  consequences, 83

crisis, 116–117, 123–124, 129, 136
  lockdown, 46, 74–75
Creative chaos, 13
Creative tension, 8–9
Creativity, orchestration, 3, 77
CRM system, 135
Cross-functionality, 135–136
Curiosity, 51, 77–78
Customer, 75–76, 81–84
  centering, 73
  centricity, 124–125
  channels, 82–83
  engagement, 74
  intelligence, 59–60
  jobs-to-be-done, 78
  preeminence, 74
  satisfaction, 124–125

D

Dalle, François, 22, 32, 39, 54–59, 78
  achievement, 122–123
  advertising perspective, 81
  company control, 34
  direct channel (inductive
    channel), 26
  do, undo, and redo philosophy, 42
  right to failure, 43
  research, 27, 85
  tension, impact, 24
Data collection, usage, 5
Data, strategic use, 84–87
Davis, Miles, 4
Dias, Georges-Edouard, 9
Digital technology, 7–8, 11–12, 74
Digital tools, deployment, 15–16
Digital transformation, 4–7, 75–80
  challenges, 85–86
  demystification, 16
  implementation, 15–16
  process, 122
Direct channel (inductive
    channel), 26
Direct-to-consumer (DTC)
  channels, usage, 46

distribution, 81–82
sales, 115
Disruption, 22
Diversity, 128
Doubt, 21, 23, 77
Do, undo, and redo (L'Oréal), 42–47
Dual innovation channel, 25–26

E

"Easy does it" approach, 33
"Eat what you cook," 125–128
E-commerce, 3–5, 9, 12
  brick-and-mortar retailers,
    competition, 83
  effort, success, 47
  environmental challenge, 126
Ecosystems, 83, 106–118
Effaclar (La Roche-Posay), 18
Em (launch), 11
Employees, motivation, 127–128
Empowerment, 132–133
Entrepreneurship, language, 15–16
eSkin, 10
Estée Lauder, 30
Ethnic diversity, 59–60
Ethnic hair products, 48
Everlane, 51
Excellence, 55

F

Facebook Messenger, 77
Failure, 11, 42–43
Fast scaling, 114–116
Feedback, 120, 121
Fenty (Rihanna), 1
Fit Culture, 61, 134
Flexlab (L'Oréal), 119–120
Foundational pillars, 1–2, 77
Founders Factory (accelerator),
  48, 53, 65
Framing, 120–121, 128–130
Friends
  advice, 95–96
  impact, 96–97

looks, sharing, 97–98
shopping, 98
solutions, 94
togetherness, 100–102

G

Global cosmetics market, 162
Globalization, 56–57
"Go Forth and Innovate", 83
Golden Triangle, 55
Google, Amazon, Facebook, and
  Apple (GAFA), 29–30
Greenpeace, 6
Grégoire, Vincent, 41
Growth-hacking, 16

H

Hero, culture, 122–123
Hieronimus, Nicolas, 128
House 99 (Beckham brand), 85
Hsieh, Tony, 76
Human-centered transformation, 71
Hypnôse Doll Eyes mascara,
  9–10

I

Icon, making, 62
Improvisation, 4, 6–13
Inclusion, 128
Incubators, 47–49
Indie brands, 1, 29
Influencer marketing,
  importance, 64–65
Information sharing, 6
Innovation, 39–44
  consumer insights, impact, 85
  dual innovation channel, 25–26
  L'Oréal approach, 43–44
  open innovation ecosystem,
    65–68
  rigor, 37, 77
  social innovation labs, 127
Innovators, MVP role, 39–42

Inoa (ammonia-free coloration products), 26
Institute for Ethnic Hair and Skin Research (L'Oréal), 60
Interdependence, 112–113

J

Japan, L'Oréal entry, 32–33
Jenner, Kylie, 64
Jobs-to-be-done, 75, 78, 85
J. Walter Thompson, 56

K

K-beauty, 84
Keats, John, 9
Key performance indicators (KPIs), 112
Kiehl's, 24, 29, 34, 53, 63, 66
  e-commerce 10
  L'Oréal acquisition, 7, 29, 49, 125
Kim Kardashian West (KKW), 1, 65
Kind of Blue (Davis), 4
Kylie Cosmetics, 1

L

La Cagoule, 22
La Maison du Bonheur (House of Happiness), 81
Lancôme, 9–10, 40, 66, 81–82
  Le Teint Particulier, launch, 49, 79
La Roche-Posay
  Effaclar brand, 18
  My Skin Track UV brand, 46–47
L'Aventure L'Oréal (Dalle), 22, 54
Lead & Enable for Simplicity (L'Oréal), 122
Learning, culture, 37, 77, 134
"Leave before it burns," 125–128
Listening with curiosity, 51, 77–78
Livestreaming, 115–116
L'Occitane en Provence, 63
Looks, sharing, 97–98

L'Oréal
  acquisitions, 63–64, 153–157
  Active Cosmetics Division, 10
  Alibaba partnership, 18, 66
  Baidu partnership, 66
  Beauty Tech Labs, 112
  brand portfolio, 159
  Citizen Day program, 127
  collective problem-solving, 130–131
  confrontation room, 24–25, 132
  Connected Beauty Institute (CBI), 11–12
  cultural legacy, importance, 77–78
  digital readiness, 114–115
  digital transformation, 16, 85–86, 133–134, 140
  distribution, 55–56
  diversity, 128
  do, undo, and redo, 42–47
  DTC sales, 115
  "easy does it" approach, 33
  e-commerce, 9, 12, 114
  ecosystem, power, 117–118
  Fit Culture, 61, 134
  Flexlab, 119–120
  global vision, 41
  "Go Forth and Innovate" approach, 83
  Hairdressing and Entrepreneurship, bachelor's degree program, 67
  history, 151–152
  Institute for Ethnic Hair and Skin Research, 60
  Nestlé, partnership, 65
  Professional Products Division, 10, 125
  Schwarzkopf, competition, 22–23
  Share & Care program, 126–127
  Sharing Beauty with All, 126
  Simplicity manifesto/program, 49, 120–122, 130–131, 133, 135
  social innovation labs, 127
  social responsibility, 126

sustainability, 126, 129–130
Technical Study Days, 67
Tencent partnership, 66
test and learn, 42, 44–45, 893
Women in Digital
    (accelerator), 53–54
L'Oréal China, 17–18, 30–31,
    116–117
L'Oréal Group, Annual General
    Meeting, 56–57
L'Oréal Hong Kong, 45
Loréalians, 13, 39–40
L'Oréalization, 60–61
L'Oréal World Cup, 135
Louis Vuitton, digital
    transformation, 14
Lower-tier cities, 31
Luk, Larry, 45
Luxury sector, 9–11

M

Machine learning, usage, 73–74
Magic Masks, 31
Makeup Genius, 11–12, 27, 49, 51–52
Marionnaud, 84
Market leaders/challengers, 28–34
Matrix, 62
Matte Shaker Lipstick, 64–65
Maybelline, 18–19, 62, 77
Meetings, 24, 28, 120, 121, 130–131
Menesguen, Marc, 9
Michelin, 14
Mininurse, L'Oréal acquisition, 31
Mistakes, overcoming, 43–44
ModiFace, 49, 51–52, 60, 63–64, 67,
    82, 84, 113
Monsavon, 38–39, 54
MVP innovator, 41
My Skintrack UV, 27–28, 46–47

N

Nailbots, 125
Natura, 63, 82

Negative capability, 9
Neiman Marcus, 24
Nestlé, 6, 65
Net-à-Porter, 51
Nice & Lovely, 60
Noah, Gayle, 112
Nordstrom, 24
NYX, 10–11, 62–63, 77, 125
Nyxification, 61–62

O

Ombré consumer blending trend, 10
Omnichannel approach, 18–19
Omnichannel partnerships, 66–67
One-way marketing, 76
Open innovation ecosystem, 65–68
Orange Is the New Black, 121
Organized chaos, 8–9, 24
Outside-in learning, 65–66
Owen-Jones, Lindsay, 23, 28–29, 34
    achievement, 122–123
    advertising perspective, 81
    department store investigations, 56
    ethnic diversity
        identification, 59–60
    failure, learning, 43
    research, 85

P

Pacific Bioscience, 44
Paris Super Liner Blackbuster,
    launch, 10
Partech International Ventures, 48
Partnerships, 67–68
Passion, science (balancing), 26–27
Perfection, 133–135
Performance, business
    insights, 85–87
Pettijean, Armand, 53
Phan, Michelle, 11
Poietis , 66
Politeness of the heart
    (Bergson), 54–59

Poulle, Marc Antoine, 124
Power balance, shift, 74
Precision marketing, 45, 80–81
Problem-solving, 130–131
Procter & Gamble, 30
Productive anxiety, 22–23
Programmatic marketing, 80
Proofs of concept, 12
Prud'homme, Christophe, 129

Q

Questioning, 24–25

R

Rakuten, 115
Redken, 62
Refined universe, 53
Resilience, 116–118
Resonance, 16–19
Rihanna, 1, 64
Rinderknech, Stéphane, 18,
     30, 31, 893
Risk, mitigation, 43
Risk-taking, usage, 80
Rochet, Lubomira (CDO),
     13–17, 60, 130
  achievement, 114
  capability sourcing, 64
  e-commerce effort, success, 47
  resonance phase, signal, 19
  role, 41–42, 46, 61
Roddick, Anita, 63
Rolex, digital transformation, 14
Rose Robot, 81
Rouge in Love, 9–10
Rozé, Frédéric, 29

S

Salon promotional activities,
     support, 67
Salonworld platform, Agon
     introduction, 10

Schueller, Eugène, 22, 37–39, 42
  business, building, 59
  Dalle replacement, 34
  disruption, 33
  patent, filing, 25–26
  politeness of the heart, 54–59
  product invention, 25
  spirit, 41
  story/legacy, 122
Schwarzkopf, competition,
     22–23
Search data, 85
Sebit, Tugcan, 133
Seed Phytonutrients, 132
Senge, Peter, 8
Sephora (LVMH), 5, 24, 63, 82, 84
Shakespeare, William, 9
Shanghai
  Exhibition Center L'Oréal event
     (2017), 30
  R&D center, opening (2005), 31
Share & Care program,
     126–127
Shared purpose, 108–109
Sharing Beauty with All, 126
Shiseido, 30
Shu Uemura, 33, 62, 77
Silicon Clichy, 19, 21
Simplicity manifesto/program, 49,
     120–122, 130–135
Singles' Day (11/11), 18, 31,
     58, 83, 115
SkinConsult AI, 73–74, 76–77
Social centricity, 92–94
Social media, 45, 89
Social networks, usage, 3
Société Française des Teintures
     Inoffensives pour Cheveux
     (French Company for Harmless
     Hair Dyes), 38
Société Générale, digital
     transformation, 14
SoftSheen, L'Oréal acquisition, 60

Sogeti, 14
Solution-focused
    collaboration, 110–111
Solutions, finding, 94
Speichert, Mark, 7
Spery, André, 38
Start-up ventures, 43
Station F (accelerator), 48, 53,
    65, 67
Status quo, challenge, 23–24
Strategic partnerships, 66
Style My Hair, 52
Stylenanda, 84
Superdrug, 84
Super Oréal Blanc, 54–55

T

Tailify, 64–65
Teams, hero role, 122–124
Technical Study Days (L'Oréal), 67
Tencent, L'Oréal partnership, 66
Tension, 27–28
Test and learn (test-and-learn), 42,
    44–47, 81, 133–135
Tmall, 18, 83, 85, 115
Top Stylist (L'Oréal), 67
Torture test (China), 58–59

U

Universalization, 56–58
Urban American Chic, 62
Urban Decay, 10, 116, 125

V

Valtech, 13
Vichy, 73–74, 77
Virtual makeover app, 11–12
Virtual platform, 46
Virtual reality (VR)
    technology, 51–52
Virtual try-on (service), 77,
    78, 115, 125

W

Watson, Emma, 10
WeChat , 18
Welch, Jack, 133
Wine Game, 134–135
Wolf, Shane, 132
Women in Digital accelerator
    (L'Oréal), 53–54
Working/practices, simplicity
    definition, 121
Worldwide leaders, 28–30

Y

YSL (L'Oréal brand), 45, 53, 62, 77
Yue Sai, 31

Z

Zappos, 51, 76, 77
Zhang, Daniel, 18, 83
Zhang, Yanyan, 118
Zviak, Charles, 28

Eugène Schueller, L'Oréal
CEO, 1909-1957

Credit : DR/ Archives L'Oréal

François Dalle, L'Oréal CEO,
1957-1984

Credit : DR/ Archives L'Oréal

Charles Zviak, L'Oréal
CEO, 1984-1988

Credit : DR/ Archives L'Oréal

Lindsay Owen-Jones, L'Oréal
CEO, 1988-2006

Dahmane / Patrimoine ou L'Oréal

Jean-Paul Agon, L'Oréal
CEO, 2006-2021

Credit : Thomas Laisné/La
Company/L'Oréal

Lubomira Rochet, Chief Digital Officer
Credit : Stéphane Gallois@tristangodefroy

The Armani Box

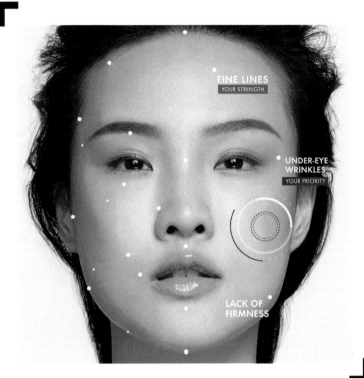

App SkinConsult

Credit : Photographers : Antoine et Charlie (Tristan Godefroy), Model : Gia (Yi-Shuang Tang) (Agence New Madison)

L'Oréal's Beauty Tech Atelier

Credit : Romain Bassene/ L'Oréal

Kérastase/Withings Device

Micro production unit for Lancôme's Teint Particulier
Credit : Dacor Productions

The Flexlab
Credit : Nathalie Oundjian

L'Oréal new hairdresser training campus
Credit : Alexis Raimbault pour L'Oréal